COUNTDOWN *to* ARMAGEDDON

Paul McGuire

CREATION
HOUSE

COUNTDOWN TO ARMAGEDDON by Paul McGuire
Published by Creation House
A division of Strang Communications Company
600 Rinehart Road
Lake Mary, Florida 32746
www.creationhouse.com

Unless otherwise noted, all Scripture quotations are
from the New King James Version of the Bible.
Copyright © 1979, 1980, 1982 by Thomas Nelson,
Inc., publishers. Used by permission.

Scripture quotations marked NAS are from the New
American Standard Bible. Copyright © 1960, 1962, 1963,
1968, 1971, 1972, 1973, 1975, 1977 by the Lockman
Foundation. Used by permission.

Scripture quotations marked NIV are from the Holy Bible,
New International Version. Copyright © 1973, 1978, 1984,
International Bible Society. Used by permission.

Scripture quotations marked KJV are from the
King James Version of the Bible.

Library of Congress Catalog Card Number: 99-76014
International Standard Book Number: 0-88419-656-9

0 1 2 3 4 5 6 VP 8 7 6 5 4 3 2 1
Printed in the United States of America

Dedication

To Kristina, Paul, Michael and Jennifer

Acknowledgments

Thank you to all the people at Creation House: Stephen Strang, Dave Welday, Rick Nash and Peg de Alminana.

Contents

SECTION III
ARE WE READY FOR WHAT IS COMING?

Introduction

Following the Comet's Trail

M Y WIFE RAN to the bedroom window in our home in Los Angeles County and shouted, "It's huge!" I said, "What's huge?" She said, "Hale-Bopp!" My three kids shouted together, "Hale-Bopp," and ran downstairs to go outside and look at the comet. When I went outside in the backyard to join them I was startled. Hale-Bopp seemed to dominate the night sky with its tail of cosmic dust trailing behind it. It looked magnificent as it displayed its cosmic fireworks show high above all the homes in the small community where we live nestled against the hills of the high desert.

Tragically, a few weeks later during Easter week,

thirty-nine members of the Heaven's Gate cult committed suicide in a mansion in Rancho Santa Fe, California. These strange cult members who died wearing black Nike running shoes believed that there was a spaceship hiding behind the Hale-Bopp comet summoning them to join that great "mothership in the sky."

Although I do not believe that in and of itself the presence of Hale-Bopp has any particular prophetic significance, there is a growing sense of the apocalyptic in our society. A Taiwanese cult proclaims that a flying saucer will come to save them, and the Solar Temple cult prepares for a mass suicide next to a volcano.

Daily the headlines of our newspapers reveal that our society and the world in which we live seem to be unraveling at the seams. Our media releases news stories of possible apocalyptic asteroid collisions; kids are shooting kids in our junior high schools; El Niño storms smash into our coastlines; and new disease outbreaks are reported daily. Even the $200 million movie, *Titanic*, reflects the growing sense of doom that pervades our society. Here in Los Angeles it was announced that beneath the Federal Building on Santa Monica Boulevard there exists a massive underground bunker to house people if a calamity strikes the city. From the quiet confines of this underground bunker, protected by a series of bank vault-type doors, government officials can monitor social unrest with television cameras strategically placed around the city.

The headlines of a Los Angeles newspaper read,

"Woman linked to occult could get death," and the story described how a "witchcraft-practicing supermarket clerk was convicted on Friday in the brutal murder of her lover's wife, a slaying that prosecutors claimed was a human sacrifice intended as a birthday gift." Tragically, these things are not isolated cases.

The problems of our world are not just sociological. It seems that our weather is out of control, and the very earth on which we stand is shaking. Thousands desert their homes as Hurricane Floyd slams into the East Coast, storms from El Niño threaten large areas of the globe and powerful earthquakes jolt Turkey, Taiwan and Mexico. A year 2000 computer bug threatens to cause chaos in cyberspace, and meterorites strike Colombia.

In the words of Charles Dickens, "It was the best of times, it was the worst of times." On one hand we have cynical rock 'n roll groups singing lyrics like "It's the end of the world as we know it, and I feel fine." On the other hand, we see over one million men from the Promise Keepers group lying prostrate on the ground in front of our nation's capital, renewing their pledges to God and their wives and asking God to spare our nation from judgment.

It is my opinion that mankind has never lived in such a unique period of history. Never before has mankind had such powerful technology in the forms of high-speed computers, genetic engineering, cloning, satellites, space travel, nuclear and biological weapons and artificial intelligence. Yet at the same time our civilization seems to be falling apart. Respected physicists like Michio Kaku believe that our world must evolve into what he calls a "Type 1" planet, or we will self-destruct. According to Kaku, the earth is currently a "Type O" civilization, which he characterizes as fundamentalist and nationalistic. He believes that we will move into a "Type 1" civilization, where we will have "planetary consciousness."[1]

However, it is not just scientists like Kaku who are calling for a global change in order to avoid our world's headlong path into self-destruction. Futurists like Alvin Toffler are calling for the end of nationalism and the creation of some kind of world state in order to save our planet. These men are joined by powerful political and economic forces that are moving behind the scenes to usher in what is now termed "world governance."[2]

THE COUNTDOWN TO ARMAGEDDON BEGINS

Through the ancient Hebrew prophets, the words of Jesus Christ and the revelation to the apostle John, the Bible predicted the very things that we are now facing as well as mankind's ill-fated attempt to deal with them. It seems that since the year 1948 when Israel was reformed as a nation, a prophetic clock has been counting down the hours.

Listed below are just a few of the major events that began around the year 1948.

- Israel reformed as a nation.
- There has been an explosion of cults, false religions and false messiahs.
- The UFO incident in Roswell, New Mexico,

occurred in 1947, and there has been a global increase in UFO sightings.

- Worldwide evangelism is taking place.
- There has been an exponential increase in computer technology.
- The atomic bomb was dropped on Hiroshima in 1945.
- In 1945, delegates from fifty nations gathered to form the United Nations.
- The spread of television and modern communications technology is evident.
- Major "earth changes" are taking place, such as the increase of earthquakes, freak weather, famines, solar storms and global environmental pollution.

THE GREAT HORROR

The human race entered a new era after 1948. Many believe that since that time period the human race is literally pressing its face against the window of what the Bible calls the Great Tribulation. (Some newer Bible translations call it the "Great Horror.") This will be a time of unprecedented trouble for Planet Earth. Earth changes of all kinds will take place in the weather, environment and society.

Even those outside the religious community are acknowledging these coming cataclysmic changes. Radio talk show host Art Bell and author Brad Steiger write in their book, *The Source,* about Indian prophecies of the

"Great Cleansing" and the "Great Purification."[3] Bell and Steiger discuss ancient North American Indian prophecies and Mayan predictions of a global cataclysm intended to purify the earth.

Section I
Signs of the Times

*The disciples came to Him privately,
saying, "Tell us, when will these things be,
and what will be the sign of Your coming,
and of the end of the age?"*

——MATTHEW 24:3, NAS

....

Is It the End
of the World As
We Know It?

F OR CENTURIES MANKIND has been speculating about
such things as the end of the world and the return
of Jesus Christ. Earthquakes, wars and famines have always been with us. However, never before in the history
of mankind have we had the technology to wipe out the
entire human race in a matter of hours. This time it's completely different. Our nation now deals with a madman
like Saddam Hussein, biochemical weapons threaten the
entire world and rogue nations like Iran have nuclear
weapons that could trigger World War III.

The entire world shuddered as India and Pakistan set
off nuclear weapons. It became even more frightened

when North Korea fired a missile over Japan. Now intelligence sources tell us that China has stolen our newest nuclear missile secrets, and both Korea and China can hit us with nukes![1] In addition, the war in Kosovo signals to us that a new world order can strike against any nation including Israel.

We no longer live in the days of Napoleon or even Adolph Hitler in which wars could be contained. We live in a brave new world of nuclear, computer and biochemical terrorism, where the whole world can be shut down in a matter of seconds.

Ancient Hebrew prophets like Daniel and Ezekiel had the capacity to see into the future and glimpse into a time when the world would be ruled by a charismatic leader the Bible calls the Antichrist, and when Russia, along with a confederation of Middle Eastern allies, would invade Israel in the last days. The prophet John, while exiled on the island of Patmos, had a terrifying vision of the future when the entire world would be plunged into what the Bible calls the Great Tribulation, and the battle of Armageddon would unfold. Jesus Christ Himself warned mankind of a future time when earthquakes, famines, wars and cults would proliferate in order to prepare people for what was to come.

Since 1948 when Israel was reformed as a nation, the world has entered a countdown period in which prophetic events rapidly unfold before our very eyes. This reality is not being observed by only those who believe in the Bible. Scientists, mystics, atheists and agnostics all seem to agree that we are entering into a watershed moment for the human race where mankind will either survive or become extinct. In fact, many in the New Age movement are warning us that the entire earth is going to enter a period of a "great cleansing" where there will be an increase in volcanoes, tidal waves, asteroid impact, disease and other phenomena that will dramatically affect life as we know it.

Although I've been a student of Bible prophecy for many years, my own interest in this subject took a dramatic turn in January of 1994 when my family was seriously affected by the Northridge earthquake. As we slept in a tent outside of our home in Southern California, I remember that many of my nonreligious neighbors came up to me and asked me if this was the "end of the world" or a "sign of the times" that Jesus Christ talked about in the Bible. I must have heard that question dozens of times in the weeks immediately following the Northridge earthquake. From that point I began to do intensive research about the prophetic signs unfolding around our world.

In the following pages I have attempted to outline some of these powerful prophetic realities. I have been privileged to share this information at major prophecy conferences and on television and radio programs that have communicated this message to millions of people around the world. My goal has never been to stir up fanaticism or to set dates. But I do believe that these prophetic signs all around us can prepare us for the return of Jesus Christ. Jesus said, "But of that day and hour no one knows, not even the angels of heaven, nor the Son, but the Father alone" (Matt. 24:36). In this passage of Scripture we are warned about setting dates.

I believe the Bible is teaching us that on one hand we are to look forward to the soon return of Jesus Christ, and we are to be spiritually ready. Yet, on the other hand we are to plan and live our lives out in such a way that if He does not return in our lifetime, we have been faithful stewards of what He has entrusted to us. This implies long-term planning, investment and preparing our children to live effectively for God in the future.

It is possible to live in the unique tension of readiness, revival and responsibility. Therefore as we examine some of the incredible prophetic events that are taking place in our lifetime, we do so responsibly and maturely.

But the day of the Lord will come like a thief, in which the heavens will pass away with a roar and the elements will be destroyed with intense heat, and the earth and its works will be burned up.

—2 PETER 3:10, NAS

....

Stormy
Weather

E L NIÑO—ANY way you look at it, the weather is getting weirder—hot spells in the winter, floods in the
desert, hurricanes, tornadoes and so on. Many meteorolo-
gists attribute this to the effects of El Niño—the warming
of ocean waters in the Pacific Ocean. In addition, some
scientists believe that the increase of winds from west to
east has actually slowed the earth's rotation, so that our
days are now two-thirds of a second longer.

It takes the earth about 23 hours, 56 minutes and
4.09053 seconds to rotate, which gives us our 24-hour
day. We orbit the sun once a year, and Planet Earth is
also moving with the sun around the center of our

galaxy, as well as moving with the galaxy as it drifts through intergalactic space. Although no one knows for sure what the total effect of the slowing of our earth could be, it is interesting to note that not only is our weather getting weirder, but the rotation of our planet in space has been affected.

BERSERK WEATHER

Recently, hundreds of fires ravaged Florida, scorching over three hundred thousand acres. Forests in Indonesia and South America have also burned down. Underground fires in Mexico have blown smoke across the border so thick that people's eyes are watering in Texas. Across the planet, fires seem to be scorching our world.

At the same time that many areas on our planet are burning, we are experiencing an increase in floods, torrential rains and hurricanes. Flooding from the Yangtze River in China has caused over $20 billion in economic loss, five million homes have been destroyed and over three thousand people have died. Typhoons pouring down record amounts of rainfall have flooded many regions. In North Korea, a severe famine partially caused by flooding has led to the death of nearly eight hundred thousand people from starvation. To help in the crisis, the United States has pledged two hundred twenty thousand tons of food, the United Nations and China have pledged another one hundred ten thousand tons of food and the European Union has offered ninety-five thousand tons of food. However, even in the middle of mass starvation, the

North Korean government continues to export over $500 million worth of missiles a year.[1]

While China is flooding, a severe drought has destroyed rice crops, causing one million people to go hungry. Due to the severe drought, people have begun to hoard water, which has caused nearly 8,800 cases of dengue and 3,300 cases of malaria.[2] In Mexico, thirty thousand people have fled into emergency shelters to escape the flooding in the state of Chiapas.

Scientists who are a part of the United Nation's Intergovernmental Panel on Climate Change (IPCC) have been watching the average global temperatures rise steadily. They predict that in the next hundred years sea levels could rise 1.6 feet, which would flood heavily populated areas from Mississippi to Bangladesh. In addition, these scientists believe that the weather will become even more extreme, producing more intense hurricanes and droughts.[3]

El Niña and El Niño have killed an estimated 2,100 people and have caused over $33 billion in property damage.[4] Last year was the warmest year since atmospheric scientists began keeping records in 1866!

WE ARE IN FOR STORMY WEATHER

Recently we have had more freak weather in our world than we have ever had before. Prior to 1988, no national insurance company ever had to pay out more than $1 billion in settlements due to weather-related disasters. However, since 1988 the insurance companies have had to shell out over $17 billion for heat wave, flood, record snowfall and drought-related problems. Many scientists believe that this volatile weather is the direct result of global warming. However, other scientists militantly disagree.

The United Nation's IPCC compiled a report by more than three hundred scientists. Containing over two thousand pages, the report suggests that between now and the year 2010, global warming will create major changes in our world. The IPCC has warned that within fifty years more than a million people a year could die from the spread of malaria, induced by global warming. These scientists suggest that disease outbreaks like cholera may be linked to global warming. In addition, the IPCC believes that rising sea levels will expose millions of people across the planet to storm damage and flooding.

Although the real cause of these weather changes is in hot dispute among scientists from MIT and other organizations, ecologists like Vice President Al Gore have been quick to use the global warming crisis to initiate a new level of governmental bureaucracy.[5]

Intelligence reports indicate that Russia now has weather modification satellites that can create tornadoes and other weather changes on our planet. Although international bodies have attempted to create treaties that disallow weather modification weapons and experimentation, all kinds of loopholes exist in these treaties.

Reportedly, the government of Malaysia has allowed weather modification experiments to be conducted in certain parts of the country. Many believe that the United States has secretly developed weather modification satellites. With the current rise in "freak-weather" patterns, one wonders if some of these weather changes are due to experimentation of weather modification weaponry.

TURNING NIGHT INTO DAY

Perhaps the most radical of all plans to change our weather is the Russian Space Regatta Consortium's plan to turn night into day. This group of companies near Moscow is planning to launch hundreds of mirrors into space that will be able to reflect sunlight from the far side of the earth and actually light up the night sky over Siberia and the Arctic. Each mirror that goes up into space will be a hundred times brighter than the moon and will be seen as far away as London, Brussels, Seattle and Quebec.

The Space Regatta Consortium plans to send up a test satellite with a powerful space mirror soon. Many scientists are concerned that this "space mirror" project will destroy balances in the ecosystem that will cause the Arctic to melt and further raise our sea levels.

In the six hundredth year
of Noah's life, in the second month,
on the seventeenth day of the month,
on the same day all the fountains of
the great deep burst open, and the
floodgates of the sky were opened . . .

—Genesis 7:11, NAS

....

3

Death by
Volcanoes

R ECENTLY I WAS vacationing with my wife, Kristina, and
my three children, Paul, Michael and Jennifer near
Mammoth Lakes, California, a five-hour drive north of Los
Angeles. It is absolutely beautiful up there with its clean
mountain air, glorious snow-covered peaks and peaceful
lakes. We rented a motor boat and went out to fish in the
middle of a lake. As I threw my line into the water, I took in a
panoramic view of the awesome mountain scenery. Although
I had heard that Mammoth Lakes was sitting right on top of a
volcano, I dismissed the thought in favor of catching a fish
that we could fry and cook with lemon for dinner.

Yet many scientists predict that within the next twenty

years Mammoth Lakes will experience a massive volcanic eruption that will make Mount St. Helens look like a Sunday school picnic. The Mammoth Lakes eruption will be something like the Krakatau volcano, which blew up with ten thousand times more force than the nuclear bomb that was dropped on Hiroshima. The sound of Krakatau going off was the loudest sound in recorded history. Gas shot twenty-five miles into the air, and giant waves went out in all directions killing tens of thousands of people. Nine hours after the volcano erupted, waves called *tsunami,* traveling at over four hundred miles an hour, roared into the beaches of Calcutta.

According to a special report in *Life* magazine, this massive volcanic eruption will have the power of a million atom bombs. It will be heard a thousand miles away—and it could happen sooner than you think.[1] We are on the verge of another major volcanic explosion.

Two thousand years ago thousands of people were buried alive by a volcanic eruption at Mount Vesuvius in Pompei. In our century alone over one hundred thousand people have been killed by volcanoes. There are currently fifteen hundred known active volcanoes with eight to twelve eruptions going off at any given moment.[2]

Could it be that it is only by God's grace these volcanoes are not suddenly erupting in full deadly force? History shows us that Pompeii was a very evil and decadent civilization. In A.D. 79, Mount Vesuvius suddenly poured out suffocating ash and poison gas while a concrete-like substance of boiling pumice hardened around the bodies of people in its path. The lesson of Pompeii has been preserved for all history, because the volcanic ash has created eerie statues of the remains of its victims. One particularly chilling image is that of a husband and wife and small child, whose bodies are molded in place like statues.

Eventually, an unrepentant mankind will enter into what the Bible calls the period of the Great Tribulation where God's wrath will be poured out. During the time just before the flood in Noah's day, Sodom and Gommorah and other societies that had become incredibly wicked were judged by God for their sins. It may well be that it is God Himself who restrains the earth from the kind of cataclysmic disaster that geologists predict will happen every six hundred thousand years.

Noah was able to view the disaster from the safety of the ark. When the Bible says, "The fountains of the great deep burst open," it seems to refer to global undersea earthquakes and massive volcanic eruptions that occurred simultaneously. During this geological upheaval, giant tidal waves or *tsunami* were rocking the ocean water back and forth. Some scientists even think that this cataclysmic event was responsible for dividing the continents from a single original land mass.

*. . . And there will be
famines, pestilences, and
earthquakes in various places.*

—MATTHEW 24:7

4

A World Facing
a Disease Crisis

I TOOK MY DAUGHTER, Jennifer, to the doctor the other day because she had a sore throat. The doctor and I got into a conversation about new strains of disease that are resistant to antibiotics. The doctor remarked that it is just a matter of time until diseases evolve that are completely resistant to antibiotics. He warned that when that happens "we will all be gone" because plagues will break out. He said major drug companies are racing to develop new drugs to combat this problem. The problem is exacerbated in Third World nations, where people abuse antibiotics by indiscriminately taking them for almost anything, helping to create strains of diseases that are immune to our most powerful drugs.

According to the World Health Organization (WHO), in the next two decades one billion people across the globe will be infected with new strains of tuberculosis, and over seventy million people will die! Those statistics are absolutely staggering and will affect even those who live in the relative safety of the United States.[1]

New pestilences are sweeping the world at an ever alarming rate. According to Dr. Cary Savitch, "One woman becomes infected with AIDS every twenty seconds world-wide. Six hundred thousand babies were born HIV-infected in 1996. Some 1.2 million AIDS orphans have been left behind in Uganda. More than four hundred thousand Americans have already died of AIDS and another one million harbor the deadly virus...According to a United Nations task force, sixteen thousand people around the world will become newly infected in the next twenty-four hours. In the United States one youth becomes infected every twenty minutes."[2]

Outbreaks of strange new diseases have become a regular news item in the media. Books like *Deadly Feasts: Tracking the Secrets of a Terrifying New Plague* by Richard Rhodes, *The Hot Zone* by Richard Preston and *Emerging Viruses: AIDS & Ebola* by Leonard G. Horowitz have become bestsellers. Oprah Winfrey was sued by the meat industry for allegedly causing meat prices to fall by talking about such things as Mad Cow disease.

In addition, as problems emerge in nations like Iran and Iraq, biological weapons such as anthrax have become household words. According to *USA Today,* "Some historians even believe that anthrax caused the fifth biblical plague of Egypt."[3]

The World Health Organization, an agency of the United Nations, recently declared that the world is facing a "global crisis" and "no country is safe from infectious diseases."[4] According to WHO statistics, diseases such as malaria and AIDS killed more than seventeen million people worldwide this past year, including nine million children.

Tuberculosis, the number one infectious disease, took 3.1 million lives last year, up from a figure of more than over 400,000 from 1993. Ten or twenty years ago scientists thought that modern antibiotics would wipe disease off the face of the earth. Now, new resistant strains of disease are breaking out all over the world. Add the problem of disease spread because of modern jet travel, and these diseases have the potential to spread all over the world overnight.

According to the WHO report, the reasons for the increase of infectious disease are factors such as poverty, population growth, pollution, antibiotic resistance, crowding and international air travel. In addition, scientists have discovered thirty new diseases, like AIDS and the Ebola virus, during the past two decades. WHO estimates that over twenty million people worldwide are currently infected with the AIDS virus.

> According to World Health Organization statistics, the world's ten leading infectious disease killers are:
>
> | DISEASE | ANNUAL DEATH RATE |
> |---|---|
> | • Acute respiratory infections | . . .4.4 million |
> | • Diarrheal diseases | . . . . .3.1 million |
> | • Tuberculosis | . . . . .3.1 million |
> | • Malaria | . . . . .2.1 million |
> | • Hepatitis B | . . . . .1.1 million |
> | • HIV/AIDS | . . . . .1 million |
> | • Measles | . . . . .1 million |
> | • Neonatal tetanus | . . . . .500,000 |
> | • Whooping cough | . . . . .335,000 |
> | • Roundworm and hookworm | . . . . .165,000[5] |

CONTAMINATION OF THE FOOD SUPPLY

Every year over eighty-one million Americans suffer from illnesses generated from bacteria in our food supply. Ninety-one hundred of these individuals die. The cost for food-borne illnesses is anywhere from $5.6 billion to $22 billion, including medical care and lost income. Hudson Foods ordered the largest meat recall in history—over twenty-five million pounds of hamburger—after it was discovered that the beef was contaminated with *E.coli 0157:H7,* which is a deadly bacteria. Raspberries imported from Mexico made thousands of school children sick because they were contaminated with the parasite cyclospora.[6]

Although government and industry are quick to hide the fact, the text of the GATT and NAFTA agreements have contributed heavily to the contamination of the world's food supply because food is now produced cheaply in Third World countries with much less stringent standards. We now have a "global garden" where food is produced all over the world, but often without the same sanitary and health standards found here in the United States. Fifty or sixty years ago most of our food was produced by local farmers on family-owned farms. Over 70 percent of outbreaks of food-borne illnesses can be traced to meat and poultry products. In addition, new food-borne disease organisms are breaking out that are resistant to antibiotics. A new and deadly form of salmonella poisoning called *Salmonella typhimurium,* or DT 104, is resistant to most antibiotics.

Scientists are now concerned about the growing contamination in the world's food supply and the inability of traditional antibiotics to kill these diseases.

When He opened the third seal,
I heard the third living creature say,
"Come and see." So I looked, and behold
a black horse, and he who sat on it
had a pair of scales in his hand.

—REVELATION 6:5

5

....

Famine

IN REVELATION 6:6 we read that a quart of wheat will be sold for a denarius. A denarius was the daily wage of the average laborer in New Testament times. The rider on the black horse is a symbol of economic collapse. During normal economic times a laborer could have purchased eight times that amount of wheat with a denarius. However, during the Great Tribulation there will be many places on Planet Earth that will suffer from massive food shortages.

Already the world grain market is in serious turmoil. World grain harvests have fallen dramatically for three years in a row. Warehouse stockpiles of grain have dropped to a dangerous level. The Food and Agriculture

Organization (FAO) of the United Nations has classified the world grain supply as very dangerously low, and prices for grain have jumped 40 percent in the past year. Many in the ecological movement believe that "the earth is striking back" because of things such as pollution and overpopulation. They believe that storms like El Niño may be the earth's revenge on humanity.

Environmentalist guru Lester Brown, who is president of the Worldwatch Institute, is calling for an "ecological Pearl Harbor" to cut population growth, which he believes is responsible for many of our current ecological problems. In an interview in the French daily newspaper *Le Monde,* Brown warned of a soon-coming planetary eco-collapse with mass starvation, disease outbreaks, social anarchy and war.

Lester Brown has been using the current grain shortage and world food crisis to call for more drastic measures to control population growth. Basically this means implementing the kind of policies that the Communist Chinese government has enforced, such as forced abortions and involuntary sterilization. It is interesting to note that Lester Brown and the Worldwatch Institute have been financed with a 1974 start-up grant of $500,000 from the Rockefeller Brothers Fund and continued funding from foundations like John D. Rockefeller and Catherine T. MacArthur, Andrew W. Mellon, Ted Turner, William and Flora Hewlett, Charles Stewart Mott and agencies such as the United Nations Environmental Program, the U.N. Population Fund, the Winthrop

Rockefeller Trust, the Pew Charitable Trust and others.

In addition, Lester Brown is a member of the Council on Foreign Relations, Zero Population Growth, Common Cause and the World Future Society. Brown is also on the advisory committee of the Institute of International Economics, which is run by C. Fred Bergsten of the Trilateral Commission, which works closely with the International Monetary Fund (IMF). The people who bankroll Brown and the Worldwatch Institute read like a Who's Who of globalist groups. They are attempting to use things like the food shortage to help further their aims toward creating a one-world government.

TERMINATOR SEEDS

> And I heard a voice in the midst of the four living creatures saying, "A quart of wheat for a denarius, and three quarts of barely for a denarius; and do not harm the oil and the wine."
>
> —REVELATION 6:6

Scientists and seed-making companies have now developed special "terminator seeds" that can only be used for one harvest and do not create any new fertile seeds. Farmers are being encouraged to buy genetically altered seeds from biotechnology companies for "super-crops." But the catch is that these farmers will not be able to use the new seeds to plant new crops. These genetically altered "terminator seeds" are good for only one crop, and then the farmer has to go back to the biotech company and buy new seeds.

There are many potential problems with these "terminator seeds." The special crops grown from "terminator seeds" could be blown about by the wind, cross with ordinary crops and wild plants and spread from species to species, irreversibly sterilizing all crops on the planet. Poor countries that rely on farming to survive cannot afford to buy new seeds every year, and their people could starve. Farmers in Third World nations who must rely on this year's seeds for next year's crops could be wiped out by the "terminator seeds."

Although there is a debate among scientists about the risks of "terminator seeds," the potential of a global catastrophe exists. By tampering with the ecosystem in such a radical way, scientists and biotechnology companies may inadvertently create the scenario in Revelation 6:6 where a global food shortage occurs.

Train up a child in the way
he should go, even when he is old
he will not depart from it.

—Proverbs 22:6, NAS

6

Decline
of the Family

THE BOOK *It Takes a Village and Other Lessons Children Teach Us* was written by Hillary Clinton—along with some help from Eleanor Roosevelt, to whom she talked with the help of New Age teacher Jean Houston. Hillary Clinton calls for the "village" to help raise our children. When Hillary Clinton uses the term "village," she is saying that the government should help raise our children.[1] The shootings in Littleton, Colorado, at Columbine High School have fueled the call for "Big Government" to step in and "micromanage" all aspects of our children's lives. There are many in government who believe that it is the government—not parents—who is responsible for raising the children.

IT TAKES A FAMILY, NOT A VILLAGE

I'm sure you have noticed by now that there is a battle for the survival of the traditional family in America. Radical extremists in Washington, D.C., the media and organizations like the National Organization of Women are powerful, and they try to tell the American people that indeed "it takes a village" to raise a family.

In their vision, the traditional parents, mother and father, are replaced by an army of social bureaucrats, social workers, pyschologists and educators who have been given the legal right to tell parents how they can raise their children. These brave new world radicals have used United Nation's treaties like the U.N. Convention on the Rights of the Child to mandate what we can teach our children about God and biblical values. But they have taken these new laws even further—they plan to have government agents, or what they like to call *home visitors,* come into our homes.

This model for "home visitation" comes under a brand-new government program paid for by your tax dollars called Healthy Families America (HFA), developed by the National Committee for the Prevention of Child Abuse. This HFA program will allow over fifty visits by government agents annually to see if parents are spanking their children or are raising their children in a "politically correct way."[2]

Now, every sane person understands that child abuse is a significant and growing problem in our society and that innocent children need to be protected from the horrors of such abuse. However, there is often a thin line between the protection of children from real child abuse and the violation of parent's rights legitimately to raise their children. The term *parens patriae,* or the "parenthood of the state," is being increasingly used to justify the intrusion of government into the family life of America. In the French Revolution, which was a revolution based on humanistic ideas, Bertrand Barere stated, "Children belong to the general family, to the state before they belong to private families." In fact, one of the concepts promoted by this revolution was that all children belong to the state and that every child should be raised by the state after age five.[3]

Do these ideas sound absolutely outrageous to you, like something that you would hear coming out of the former Soviet Union or Communist China? Nevertheless, there is an elite group of educators and political leaders here in the United States who believe the exact same thing. In fact, these dangerous ideas of the French Revolution began to enter into the consciousness of America's political elite as far back as the 1840s when the Reform School movement was launched, which believed that parents were unworthy of properly educating their children. In 1930, during President Herbert Hoover's White House Conference on Child Health and Protection, the idea was raised that a child was the "State's child" and needed to be a citizen of a world community that was moving toward unity.[4]

The United Nations Convention on the Rights of the

Child, which has already become law in over 150 nations, takes this concept of *parens patriae* and gives the United Nations full legal authority to control and regulate family life according to its humanistic belief system. What this means in practical terms is that the government will have the right to tell you how to raise your children, and it will have the power to dictate to you what kind of moral, ethical and religious beliefs you can teach your children.

Currently the U.N. Convention on the Rights of the Child is being sent to the Senate and has the full support of the National Education Association (NEA), the National Council of Churches, Planned Parenthood, the Girl Scouts of America, the Children's Defense Fund and some of the most powerful people in Washington, D.C.

Nobel Prize Laureate Dr. Jose Ramos-Horta of East Timor, while speaking at the Children's Rights Congress, said that the Children's Rights Convention "challenges the dichotomy between the privacy of the family and the public domain of the State and its instrumentalities. The Convention disaggregates the rights of the children from the rights of families and constitutes children as independent actors with rights..."[5]

Basically, Dr. Jose Ramos-Horta was saying that the United Nations or the "State" now will have the ultimate authority over our children—not the parents!

YOU'RE NOT OK, AND I AM NOT OK

The title of a best-selling book, *I'm OK—You're OK*, sums up one of the great lies in our society—the belief that all people are basically good. Now, I don't know how anybody in their right mind could hold that belief in light of the evidence. After all, on the news every day we read about a steady parade of mass murderers, serial rapists, child abusers, drug dealers, violent criminals, white-collar crimes and political corruption. If everybody is OK, then why is the world in such a mess?

Humanists would tell us that all of this is due to a lack of education and proper upbringing. That's why Hillary Clinton wants to have the government help us raise our children. She wants to send an army of social workers, teachers, psychologists and bureaucrats into our living rooms to help us raise our families. But the real problem with people is not their lack of education or environment. The real problem is their human nature!

The Bible teaches us that human nature is fallen, self-centered and sinful. That is an accurate description of mankind. What we need is not psychotherapy; we need a Savior to save us from our real state of sinfulness. Dr. Karl Menninger, in his book titled *Whatever Became of Sin?*, stated that modern man has lost his sense of shame and guilt over what is sin. Instead we rationalize away everything. Every wrongdoing is attributed to genetics, psychological illness, parents or the environment. Nobody is responsible for his behavior anymore, and as a result we have moral anarchy.

The bottom line is that I'm not OK, and neither are you. Each of us needs a Savior. We need to be cleansed of our sins by the Lamb of God who takes away the sins of the world. The reason so many people are depressed and anxious in our society is because things are not right in their lives. They don't need to medicate themselves or rationalize things away. They need to come before a loving Savior and ask for forgiveness and cleansing.

Jesus Christ didn't just come down here "on a lark" to be crucified on a cross. He came to earth to be the Savior of mankind and to take away the sins of the world. The only way He could do this was to take these sins upon Himself on the cross. In a very real sense, Jesus Christ absorbed into His own being all the sins of mankind— the lies, selfishness, cruelty, perversion, violence, murder, greed, lust and darkness of the human race. But the only way that you can receive forgiveness by God is to accept Christ's work on the cross into your heart by faith.

THE SEXUAL EXPLOITATION OF CHILDREN

There were over twelve hundred delegates at a recent meeting of the World Congress Against Commercial Exploitation of Children in Stockholm. One expert who spoke at the meeting was a priest who said that on any given night a million children are offered in sex service to adults. Can you imagine the absolute horror of more than a million children being sexually abused each night by perverted adults?

A day of judgment is coming for the wicked; a loving and just God will not allow this outrage to continue on forever. He is giving mankind a chance to repent of their sins and turn to Christ for forgiveness. But the time is rapidly approaching when He will put a stop to all the horrors and degradation.

According to the World Congress Against the Sexual Exploitation of Children, there is multibillion-dollar illegal sex market in child prostitution. Many are children who have been kidnapped and sold into sexual slavery. In regions such as Central and Eastern Europe and some of the poorer nations of the world, children sell themselves so that they can buy the products advertising and entertainment media encourage. In other words, they sell their bodies so that they can buy designer shoes and jeans.

Americans and Western Europeans are paying customers for this kind of sexual exploitation and are a link between tourism and the child sex trade. Americans fly into Asia and Latin America in order to have sex with children. Things have gotten so bad that an organization called End Child Prostitution in Asian Tourism (ECPAT) is keeping a computer database on sex abusers from America, Germany, England and Australia.

In case we think that rampant child pornography is strictly a foreign problem, there is a literal army of pedophiles here in our own nation. Pro-life activist Randall Terry recently launched a controversial crusade against child pornography in our nation when he urged listeners of his nationally syndicated radio program, *Randall Terry Live,* to go into Barnes and Noble bookstores and rip up books by Jacque Sturgess, whose photographic books contain sexually exploitive pictures of young children.

On the front page of my local newspaper was the picture of a Little League baseball coach who was still coaching baseball even though he had been arrested for molesting a young person. Somehow his criminal record was discovered, and the paper decided to "blow his cover." The tragedy is that there are hundreds of thousands of child molesters in our nation who individually molest hundreds of children during their lifetimes. Modern psychology is ill-equipped to deal with the depravity in the sinful nature of man's heart. Fallen man is prey to sinful desires that only the cross of Jesus Christ can conquer.

KIDS KILLING KIDS

Our government-run educational system, which has rejected Judeo-Christian values and replaced prayer in schools with New Age beliefs, political correctness, the giving out of condoms and values clarification, is breaking down. Kids are now killing kids in our public schools all across the country. In Westside Middle School in Arkansas an eleven-year-old and thirteen-year-old dressed in camouflage outfits opened fire on their fellow students with rifles, killing five. Prior to that three students were killed in Paducah, Kentucky, and there were additional murders of students in Alaska and other states. Columbine High School in Littleton, Colorado, and the killing of Christian college students in a church in San Antonio, Texas, by a gunman who hated Christians are only the latest in a series of tragedies.

In all fairness, you cannot hold the school system entirely responsible for these tragedies. Although the schools clearly amplify the problem because they teach humanism, the root of the problem lies in our families and culture. Many kids come from troubled homes; the television and movies they watch are filled with sex and violence. From the White House down to the schoolhouse moral values are no longer important. Yet the more the system breaks down, the more government programs will be developed to solve the problem. These programs will only exacerbate the problem, because the real problem is spiritual.

THE GOVERNMENT BECOMES THE PARENT

At the J. T. Lambert Intermediate School in East Stroudsberg, Pennslyvania, fifty-nine eleven-year-old girls were herded into the school nurse's office and forced to submit to a complete genital exam without their parents knowledge or consent. Many of the girls left the nurse's office in tears, and several girls attempted to escape out a nearby window. The situation became so outrageous that the Rutherford Institute, a Christian legal defense team, was called in to intervene on behalf of some of the parents.[6]

Homeschoolers Leonard and Teresa Vandenburg of New Mexico were investigated by the New Mexico Children, Youth and Family Services Department (CYFS) for child abuse. Although the Vandenburgs were completely innocent of any such charge, the government continued to harass them because they wanted to homeschool their children for religious reasons. In fact, the real reason that the government was investigating them had nothing to with child abuse; it was because the government did not approve of their desire to give their children a religious education.

On October 21, 1996, Leonard Vandenburg was arrested and handcuffed while his home was searched without a warrant. Leonard Vandenburg was imprisoned at the Chaves County Jail. Although social workers for the New Mexico Children, Youth and Family Services Department found no evidence of child abuse, and the Vandenburgs received a $200,000 settlement from the state, they had to put up with costly harassment and a violation of their civil rights before they finally were given an audience with New Mexico Governor Gary Johnson and vindicated.

Tragically, cases of government abuse and intrusion into families are flooding the courts all over the nation as federal, state and local authorities in increasing numbers interfere with the rights of parents. The problem has become so large that Representatives Steve Largent (R-OK) and Charles Grassley (R-IA) created the Parents Rights and Responsibilities Act to protect parental authority from intrusion by the government. The purpose of the Parents Rights and Responsibilities Act is to protect the right of parents to direct the upbringing of their children as a fundamental right.[7]

FROM CRADLE TO GRAVE

There is a plan at work to remold the entire American system. One of the key components of that plan is to allow the government to select your child's career at a very young age during his or her education. It sounds like something out of a George Orwell totalitarian novel, doesn't it? Yet, a series of "career/workforce bills" such as the Careers Act H.R. 1617, which was overwhelmingly approved by the House and the Senate, and the Workforce Development Act (S. 143) passed with bipartisan support and call for a radical transformation of our present educational system. In a nutshell, these bills will give government, through the school system, the power to choose your child's career![8]

When the public finally got wind on what this "School to Work" program was all about, it began to pressure many of its elected officials to overturn this insidious program. Representative Henry Hyde (R-IL) began sounding the alarm and urging his fellow political leaders to repeal the legislation. The NEA Goals 2000 program, the Outcome Based Education program and the new School to Work program are attempting not only to indoctrinate our children but also to select their future careers. Computer files will be gathered on all students and sent to national career centers so that careers can be developed for each student.

A key player in all this is Marc Tucker, who along with David Rockefeller, John Sculley, David Hornbeck and others has worked with the Clinton Administration in developing a plan to completely change the culture, attitudes, values, norms and accepted ways of doing things. In other words, these people have a plan to indoctrinate, program and brainwash our youth to fit into the mold that they have laid out for them. They want to create a "seamless system" that begins in the home and continues through school and into the workplace.

Does this all sound too far-fetched? Too conspiratorial? What you have to understand is that a massive power grab is going on for our society behind the scenes that will directly affect you and your family.

WHAT THEY HAVE IN MIND
FOR YOUR CHILDREN

President Clinton's proposal for a national education standards test is a ploy to control the curriculum of both public and private schools from the federal level. The purpose of the test is not about "standards" or excellence. It's about controlling the educational agenda and values and beliefs children are being taught. Here are some of the plans the "educrats" have for your children.

1. Character education

This really means federally approved attitudes regarding things such as sexual diversity. The government wants to be in the business of teaching your children federally approved values and beliefs. It is important to note that many of these beliefs will be in direct contradiction to Judeo-Christian and biblical values.

2. Political correctness

The government wants your children to be indoctrinated into a politically correct way of thinking. It would not be politically correct to say that salvation is only through Jesus Christ or that homosexuality is a sin.

3. Good citizens

Children must hold politically correct beliefs. They must be good global citizens—not patriotic Americans. They must embrace humanistic belief systems that teach there is no God and that we are all just citizens of Planet Earth.

There is a specific game plan at work here. What is happening in education is no accident. At the very top of the educational and governmental establishments are an elite group of people who want to set up a radical new kind of society and government. To these people your Christian or patriotic beliefs are archaic. They have written you off, and they are attempting to go around you to indoctrinate your children.

THE DAYS OF NOAH AND THE DAYS OF LOT

And as it was in the days of Noah, so it will be also in the days of the Son of Man: They ate, they drank, they married wives, they were given in marriage, until the day that Noah entered the ark, and the flood came and destroyed them all. Likewise as it was also in the days of Lot: They ate, they drank, they bought, they sold, they planted, they built; but on the day that Lot went out of Sodom it rained fire and brimstone from heaven and destroyed them all.

Even so it will be in the day when the Son of Man is
revealed.

—LUKE 17:26–30

Jesus Christ compared the days immediately preceding
His return to the days of Noah and the days of Lot. Jesus
Christ said that the same sociological conditions would
be present when He returned as they were in Noah's
days and Lot's days. Exactly what were those conditions?
In both cases business was going as usual. People were
marrying, partying, doing business and living their lives
oblivious to the destruction that was coming upon them.
In Genesis 6:5 we see something else that ~~what~~ was
going on in Noah's time: "Then the LORD saw that the
wickedness of man was great in the earth, and that every
intent of the thoughts of his heart was only evil continu-
ally." Here we discover that the time of Noah was a time
when mankind had become exceedingly wicked and evil.

Genesis 6:11–12 says, "The earth also was corrupt before
God, and the earth was filled with violence. So God
looked upon the earth, and indeed it was corrupt; for all
flesh had corrupted their way upon the earth." In Noah's
time men had become violent and corrupt, and God was
going to judge them for their corruption.

Genesis 19:1–29 gives us the account of how God sent
two angels to rescue Lot and his family before He
destroyed Sodom and Gomorrah. Earlier in Genesis 18:20,
when talking to Abraham who is interceding for Sodom in
prayer, God says, "Because the outcry against Sodom and
Gomorrah is great, and because their sin is very grave…"

In the days of Lot, men had become corrupt and wicked. We see a glimpse into that corruption when we see the men of Sodom banging on the door of Lot's house and demanding to have sexual relations with the angels. Even after Lot, in desperation, offers his two daughters for their sexual gratification, the men became further enraged and were going to homosexually rape both Lot and the angels. However, the two angels supernaturally blinded the men and led Lot and his family out of Sodom before God destroyed it. Tragically, Lot's wife disobeyed God and looked back, and she was turned into a pillar of salt.

In both the case of Noah's culture and of Lot's culture, we read how society had become corrupt and debased to such a point that God had to judge it. Our world has become as corrupt and wicked as in the times of Noah and Lot. Our news media gives us daily reports of children murdering their parents, young children murdering other children, the rape of infants, grisly murders, serial killers, sexual perversions and other crimes.

THE VAMPIRE RAPIST

Atrocities have become so outrageous in our society that we have become numb. Each new day brings an outrageous horror. Even as I write this, prison officials are seeking to release John Crutchley, known as the "Vampire Rapist." Crutchley was convicted of picking up a nineteen-year-old California woman who was hitchhiking in 1985. After kidnapping and raping her, over an eighteen-hour-period he drained and drank nearly half her blood using surgical equipment. Women in local communities are terrified because he is going to be released.

The frightening thing is that this level of atrocity is not unique in our society. Daily we are assaulted with news of violence, perversion and degradation. We are in the kind of moral free fall that characterized the time of Noah and the days of Lot. At a certain point God is going to send judgment upon our world. However, as in the days of Noah and Lot, He is going to deliver His people before the full extent of His judgment falls.

*Let everyone be on guard
against his neighbor, and do not
trust any brother; because every
brother deals craftily.*

—JEREMIAH 9:4, NAS

Attacks on
Privacy

L ET'S FACE IT, all of us want clean rivers, clean air, beautiful parks, sunshine and pure food and water. No sane person wants to turn the earth into a junk heap. Certain laws, regulations and acts need to be passed in order to insure a clean environment. However, the radical environmental movement has a Trojan horse. They understand that just about everybody wants to end pollution. They use that legitimate desire as a Trojan horse to gain acceptance and trust. But their agenda goes far beyond stopping pollution. They want to use their movement's thesis to establish a wide range of social agendas from population control to governmental takeover of private property.

When the Antiwar movement died a couple of decades ago, leftist social activists needed a new movement to hitch their wagon to, and so they jumped on the Environmental movement in order to build a cause that would attract dollars and people. But the real purpose behind the Environmental movement and the Antiwar movement was to create a new social order based on selected leftist and humanistic beliefs.

Despite its public facade of the friendly naturalist wearing camping shorts and hiking boots, the Environmental movement has some pretty ugly skeletons in its closet. One involved famed author Jack London, who wrote such books as *The Call of the Wild*. In an article in *Reason* magazine titled "Call of the Whites—The skeleton in environmentalism's closet is nature," Charles Paul Freund writes, "*White Fang* author Jack London believed the call of the wild beckoned the white race to achieve its savage destiny." In his article, Freund talks about the German nature—mysticism that evolved into the National Socialism of the Nazis. It seems that within the beginnings of the modern ecological movement were men who used nature as a basis for racism where only the fittest would survive.[1]

THE WETLANDS GESTAPO

In an article in the *Wall Street Journal* titled "The Wetlands Gestapo," writer Max Boot details an account of how an honest American businessman was sentenced to twenty-one months in jail and over $1 million in fines for the crime of creating a scenic pond for people to enjoy out of unuseable wetlands.[2] Boot writes, "To any rational person what Mr. Wilson did was an improvement—replacing some forbidding, damp woods with lakes and open spaces that attract wildlife and local residents alike."

According to the *Wall Street Journal,* "This son of an Irish rebel who fought against British rule alongside Michael Collins won't go quietly: 'If the good Lord gives me the time, I'll be back to fight this battle against the subversion of our basic constitutional rights by the government.'"

THE GREAT GOVERNMENT LAND GRAB

The environmental movement has worked hand in hand with the federal government in grabbing over 4.7 million acres of forest land in states like Arizona and New Mexico. The U.S. Fish and Wildlife Service, along with the Environmental Protection Agency, is attempting to establish a ruling that will stop all logging and remove 80 percent of the cattle. The result will be that thousands of miners, ranchers and loggers will be put out of work, along with the tens of thousands of the people they hire, in order to protect the Mexican spotted owl!

The government and the environmentalists have already destroyed entire economies in Washington, Oregon, Idaho and Northern California in order to protect the habitat of the Northern spotted owl. The federal government claims to own up to 80 percent of the land in some Western states, and yet they want to grab more land. Things have gotten so bad that a "Sagebrush Rebellion II" has sprung up in counties all over the West declaring that the federal government has no legitimate right to their land.

But the question should arise, "What is the real motive for the government to be seizing so much land?" Many in the federal government believe that people are just a "biological resource" and must be managed in order to protect the ecosystem. Environmental groups, the Environmental Protection Agency and the Federal Bureau of Land Management are trying to pass an Eco System Protection Act. This act would go far beyond the Endangered Species Act and would develop human population policies. In other words, there would be governmentally regulated population sizes of geographic areas. For example, the government would have the power to determine how many people could live near Yellowstone Park or Santa Barbara, California.

Under this Eco System Protection Act the government would have the right to seize private property, control population and determine what kind of businesses can operate in any location. In short, under the guise of environmentalism, the government is given the power to regulate and direct all details of the people's lives—just as governments in China, Cuba and Russia have the power to do.

BIODIVERSITY AND THE WILDLANDS PROJECT

The U.N. Convention on Biodiversity, which was signed by Bill Clinton in 1993, is an attempt to mandate the implementation of a radical plan developed by ecologists called the Wildlands Project. Although the Senate refused to ratify this U.N. treaty, President Bill Clinton has used executive orders to get around the Senate, and much of this plan is now being put into action. This master plan is an agenda designed to transform a large portion of the United States into an enormous "eco-park." Wildlands was the dream of the founder of the eco-terrorist group Earth First, headed by Dave Foreman. Foreman would like to see us get back to the kind of civilization America had in 1492 before it was populated by Europeans.

Dave Foreman is against Judeo-Christian beliefs, technology, private property and individual rights. Although the Clinton Administration probably does not realize the full extent of Foreman's vision, his critics call the Wildlands Project nothing less than the end of industrial civilization.

UNITED NATIONS WORLD HERITAGE SITES

On January 19, 1996, President Bill Clinton signed Executive Order (EO) 12986, which helped empower the International Union for Conservation of Nature and Natural Resources (ICUN). The ICUN is used by the United Nations to promote a global environmental policy. The ICUN helped to promote what is called the U.S. Government's Man and Biosphere Program (MAB) and the World Heritage Convention. These programs are designed to give the United Nations control over certain designated sites in the United States such as Yellowstone Park. To date more than forty-seven of these Biosphere Reserves and more than twenty World Heritage Sites in the United States and around the world have been created.[3]

Sites such as Yosemite, Yellowstone, Grand Canyon,

51

Statue of Liberty, Carlsbad Caverns and other areas are now designated World Heritage sites. Through a series of complex treaties and new laws, both federal and state governments are required to obey United Nation mandates regarding these lands. It appears that all of these programs are attempts by the United Nations to extend its control over national governments. During the United Nation's Earth Summit in 1992 in Rio de Janeiro, a plan called *Agenda 21* was unveiled, which uses ecological issues as a means of furthering global government.

Big Brother Is Watching

Did you know that there is an electronic file on you and your family? Information is kept on almost every person in industrial societies and is computerized in thousands of databases by private industry and the government. The CIA and the National Security Agency, along with the Department of Justice and the Department of Defense, signed a memorandum of understanding in 1993 titled "Operations Other Than War and Law Enforcement" in order to go into partnership in sharing electronic surveillance technology.

In addition, computer and electronics companies are expanding into new markets originally developed for the military such as E-systems, Electronic Data Systems (founded by Ross Perot) and Texas Instruments that are now in the business of selling computer surveillance equipment to state and local governments. This new technology is also being sold to oppressive governments like

China, Thailand and Turkey who are attempting to stop all political dissent in their countries.

Originally technology like computerized fingerprints, ID cards, electronic dossiers, biometrics, video cameras with face recognition and other technology were used only on criminals, illegal immigrants, welfare recipients and members of the military. But there are now massive computers that track people of different religious beliefs, political persuasion—even ordinary middle-class people. These data bases are loaded with information on your spending and buying habits. These computers can instantly identify your political beliefs, your religious beliefs, even your hobbies and interests.

Like it or not, you leave a data shadow everywhere you go, and there are numerous companies attempting to analyze what you do in your spare time, what magazines you read, where you go on vacation, what television programs you watch and your political or nonprofit contributions.

THE GLOBAL SURVEILLANCE SYSTEM

A couple of decades ago, Dr. Francis Schaeffer warned that in order to manage the social chaos brought about by the rejection of Judeo-Christian values, governments across the globe would have to become more authoritarian.[4] Many people simply do not understand how far down the road we have come toward that end. One of the new technologies recently brought to light that signals the rise of authoritarianism is a global surveillance system called ECHELON. ECHELON allows intelligence agencies around the world to monitor telephone calls, E-mail, telex communications and other communications through an advanced global computer system.[5]

ECHELON's giant computers indiscriminately intercept large quantities of communications and search for messages of interest while rejecting unwanted ones. A global chain of secret interception facilities taps into all major international telecommunication systems and satellites. Interestingly, ECHELON targets nonmilitary systems that include governments and business as well as selected individuals. Powerful computers sift through millions of messages, simultaneously looking for key words, names, subjects and locations.

Intelligence agencies like the National Security Agency (NSA), Government Communications Headquarters in Britain (GCHQ), Communications Security Establishment in Canada (CSE), Defense Signals Directed in Australia (DSD) and other organizations are involved.[6]

IDENTIFICATION NUMBERS

When the Social Security card came out in 1938, we were told that this number would only be used for the purpose of identifying workers eligible for retirement benefits. Then in 1961, the IRS began using the Social Security number for income taxes. Soon numerous other agencies began using it. Today your Social Security number serves as a central identifying number for credit, employment and countless other purposes. In a very real sense, we have all become numbers.

What a lot of people don't know is that hidden in the twenty-two-thousand page World Trade Organization/ GATT documents in Section 742 there is now a requirement for every newborn baby to get a special new taxpayer identification number at birth. The next step will be the implementation of a national identification card that all citizens will be required to carry. This identification card will be in the form of a computerized smart card that will contain all kinds of personal information. This computerized smart card is already in distribution in Thailand. Thailand has the Thailand Central Population Database identification card system, which was designed by Control Data Systems located in the United States.

The repressive government of Thailand uses this ID card, which is linked to an electronic data base that keeps files on the entire population, to supply such information as birth date, political party, fingerprints, facial imaging, tax information, criminal records, gun registration, religious beliefs and other information. Such technology is going to be used all over the Third World and in First World nations. It is just a matter of time before a national identification card is used here in the United States.

It is important to understand just how pervasive computerized control is going to be in the future. Can you just imagine a room filled with bureaucrats who are watching a giant television screen showing a satellite map of the United States? Someone keys in your Social Security number, and all of a sudden the satellite begins to zoom in on your state, your city, your street and your home from its orbit high in the earth's atmosphere. Suddenly you see a close-up image of yourself going out your front door and putting your keys in your car to go to work.

Then personal data about you and your family shows up on another screen. Your income, your political beliefs, your religion, hobbies, where you work, psychological profile and other data can be seen by all. Does this all sound far-fetched? In reality, all that technology is available and in use now.

In capturing the Unabomber, the FBI monitored his cabin with close-up satellite photos. In the Oklahoma City bombing, immediately after the bombing the FBI had close-up footage of people from phone booths near the federal building. These photos were taken by satellite from high above the earth's atmosphere.

SMART CARDS AND SMART CARPETS

Smart cards, or "stored value cards," are already here. They are like electronic traveler's checks, and they can be used to buy items ranging from cheeseburgers to telephone calls. During the Olympic Games in Atlanta over one million of these smart cards were distributed to the international community gathered to watch the events.

Prestigious magazines like *Scientific American* have done detailed reports of the new technology. In an article entitled "Smart Cards" by Carol H. Fancher, the magazine outlined how current "smart card" technology is being used. For example, VisaCash released over one million smart cards to various Olympic sites, transit systems and thousands of retail outlets in Atlanta. In Spain over forty million Social Security identification cards will be issued by the year 2001. These cards will contain personal history and medical history that can be verified by a stored fingerprint. In Germany eighty million health insurance cards have been issued. These cards started out as simple ID cards. The European Union has begun issuing smart cards in an ongoing program.[7]

Here in the United States plans are underway for a national identification card and a national health card. Before long, every citizen in the United States will be required to carry a smart card that contains an electronic dossier on his or her life. In Thailand, citizens are required to carry smart cards that contain, among other things, information on religious affiliation, political party, education, health information and any criminal records. Already, the American military has issued MARC cards (Multi-Technology Automated Reader Card) that military personnel use to access meals and medical care.

Just when you thought it was safe to walk across our rugs, a new technology has been developed called the "smart carpet." Messel, a Finnish engineering company, has developed a carpet that monitors the breathing and pulse of someone lying on it. With special "intelligent fibers" the carpet is capable of receiving all kinds of information about people who are in a room.

As the Armageddon clock counts down, not only is this generation forced to deal with attacks from within government, but attacks from outside groups are also increasing.

And you will be hearing
of wars and rumors of wars.

—MATTHEW 24:6, NAS

8

Clueless on
Terrorism

C HIP BECK, A retired Navy commander and former CIA
station chief, stated in an editorial in the *Los Angeles
Times* that "the public needs to be prepared for what may
be a long and bloody battle when the bombers strike
back." Beck writes:

> Imagine downtown Los Angeles, New York or Wash-
> ington, where 100,000 inhabitants, from garbage
> collectors to CEOs, in kindergarten classes to
> nursing homes, suddenly without warning begin
> drowning in their own bodily fluids or suffocating
> on swollen tongues as mucous pours out from every
> orifice...people convulsing so violently that internal

organs are displaced and then shut down in terrifying manifestations of agony.[1]

Beck warns in this article of the very real retaliation by terrorist groups. Over and over again in this editorial, this intelligence expert warns that "the world is more dangerous than Americans realize."

OSAMA BIN LADEN

An Arabic newspaper in London ran a quote from terrorist leader Osama bin Laden, which said, "The ruling to kill Americans and their allies...civilian and military is a duty for every Muslim. We...with God's help...call on every Muslim to kill the Americans." The U.S. government is taking the threats of the forty-two-year old terrorist leader Osama bin Laden very seriously, and they are beefing up security at airports and embassies around the world.

Osama bin Laden has assets of more than $250 million from a family construction business in Saudi Arabia. Laden has helped to establish more than six hundred terrorist training camps around the world. He has been implicated in the World Trade Center bombing and other terrorist attacks. In a State Department paper titled "Overview of State-Sponsored Terrorism...Patterns of Global Terrorism," Osama bin Laden claimed to have been involved in the incident involving U.S. soldiers in Yemen, in attacks in Somalia, in the assassination attempt on Egyptian President Mubarak and with attacks against the U.S. military in Saudi Arabia. In addition, bin Laden has been implicated in the bombings of the U.S. embassies in Nairobi and Tanzania.

The U.S. cruise missile attacks against Khartoum were targeted against bin Laden's operations. But the real danger of Osama bin Laden's activities lies in domestic terrorism. Although the vast majority of the six million Muslims living in the United States are law-abiding citizens, bin Laden does have sympathizers and operatives here inside the United States. The goals of terrorists like bin Laden are the destruction of the Jewish state of Israel and the destruction of the United States, because it is pro-Israel. Terrorists like bin Laden consider citizens of the United States to be "infidels" and worthy of destruction.

WAG THE DOG

In the movie *Wag the Dog,* the president of the United States is in trouble because of a sexual scandal. To diffuse the issue he starts a war to take the public's mind off his actions. The Bill Clinton scandal seems to be reality imitating art. Just days after the Monica Lewinsky scandal broke, the State Department and the White House began announcing plans to attack Saddam Hussein in Iraq. On the day Monica Lewinsky was scheduled to testify in the Senate, President Clinton ordered a massive air strike against the terrorist camps of the men responsible for the bombings of U.S. embassies in Kenya and Tanzania. Although no one can say for sure what his intent was, the coincidences to the movie *Wag the Dog* are uncanny. In addition, the war in Kosovo has provided an excellent diversion from the Chinese spying scandals here in the United States.

Remembering when Saddam Hussein fired Scud missiles into Israel during Operation Desert Storm, many in Israel have been responding to recent news by breaking out their gas masks in case of a missile attack by Iraq. It seems we have entered into a kind of surreal world where the entire planet can be brought to the brink of World War III in an instant.

But this time the stakes are global. The Middle East is not the kind of place you want to play at politics. Our nation and the rest of the world are very vulnerable to an attack by a foreign terrorist like bin Laden.

A COMING BIOLOGICAL WARFARE ATTACK AGAINST THE UNITED STATES?

It's just a matter of time until America gets hit with a biological terrorist attack from some kind of terrorist group. The United States government is taking this very seriously and has been preparing major U.S. cities for just such a scenario. Perhaps you have seen pictures in the news media of teams of doctors dressed in what looks like white astronaut's outfits and conducting training exercises against biowar strikes. Richard Preston, in his new book *The Cobra Event,* outlines what could happen in a biological warfare attack. Preston believes that one of the most potent forms of biological warfare is the smallpox virus, which literally burns the skin off the body.[2]

Investigators from the Centers for Disease Control and Prevention are looking into the possibility that the encephalitis outbreak in New York, which has been called "West Nile-type virus," could be an act of bioterrorism.[3]

The National Guard is developing ten reaction teams to respond in the event that U.S. cities and towns are attacked by terrorists using anthrax and other chemical and biological weapons. Here in the United States we have already been hit by terrorist bombings of the World Trade Center and the federal building in Oklahoma City. In Tokyo a nerve gas attack by a freakish religious cult killed twelve and seriously injured over 5,500 people. According to Secretary of Defense William S. Cohen, "This is not something that is a scare tactic. It is reality, so we have to be prepared."[4] The Defense Department recently asked Congress if they could have $200 million in order to build a "mock" city as a training ground for a biological warfare attack. These special "RAID" teams— an acronym for Rapid Assessment and Initial Detection of biological attacks—will consist of twenty-two soldiers and have an annual budget of $49 million. However, this is just the tip of the iceberg regarding just how seriously our government takes the threat of biological warfare.

On March 3, 1998, Secretary of Defense William S. Cohen announced his decision to vaccinate U.S. military personnel deployed in the Arabian Gulf region against the biological warfare agent *anthrax*. The immunization will consist of six inoculations over an eighteen-month period.

Experts from the Centers for Disease Control and

Prevention in Atlanta, Georgia analyzed the effects of *Bacillus Anthracis, Brucella Melitensis* and *Francisella Tularensis* should they be released in the form of an aerosol spray in the suburbs of a major city. They predicted that the economic impact of a bioterrorist attack could range from $477.7 million per one hundred thousand persons to $26.2 billion per one hundred thousand persons infected. In addition, the tragedy in human lives as a result of the effects of such an attack could bankrupt health organizations and local governments.[5]

They did not repent of . . .
their sorceries.

—Revelation 9:21

Drugs, the Occult
and a Declining
Morality

M ANY YEARS AGO rock singer Bob Dylan sang those famous words, "Everybody must get stoned." Well, not everybody gets stoned. The word *sorceries,* mentioned in Revelation 9:21, comes from the Greek word *pharmakeia,* from which we get *pharmacy* or *pharmacist.* The word *sorcery* describes the use of medicine or drugs. As we get closer to the tribulation period we are seeing the use of drugs escalate to an all time high across the globe.

During the same week that Senator Fred Thompson opened the hearings on Campaign Finance Reform, a number of leading U.S. magazines ran full-page ads for the drug Prozac, encouraging people to take the drug if they are depressed. At the same time, dominant media in our country was deliberately ignoring the Senate hearings, which attempted to uncover how the Chinese and other foreign governments were attempting to control our foreign policy. Leading news magazines selling Prozac—it's like something out of Aldous Huxley's novel *Brave New World*. To make matters worse, doctors are prescribing Prozac in increasing numbers to children and teenagers!

In the United States alone, illegal drug use is a $75-billion-a-year industry. In fact, the drug problem is so serious that most experts say that the "war on drugs" is completely lost. Men like economist Milton Friedman and former Secretary of State George P. Shultz have actually called for the legalization of drugs here in the United States. According to FBI statistics, 1.3 million arrests are made each year for drug offenses. In addition, 750,000 arrests are made each year involving drug-related crimes of murder, robbery, rape and assault.

The use of psychedelic drugs like LSD and narcotics like heroin is at an all-time high for teenagers. Fifth graders in our public school system think rock legend Kurt Cobain of Nirvana is a hero. Cobain was a heroin addict who committed suicide. The younger generation's idols are filled with heroin-addicted rock stars like Shannon Hoon of Blind Mellon who, while addicted to heroin, died from a heroin overdose. Dave Navarro of the Red Hot Chili Peppers recently kicked heroin, and Jimmy Chamberlin was kicked out of the Smashing Pumpkins

band for using heroin, along with late keyboardist
Jonathan Melvoin. Michael Hutchenence, lead singer of
the group INXS, was found dead in his Ritz Carlton Hotel
room after hanging himself. Members of the group had
reportedly abused drugs.

The heroin craze is absolutely staggering among rock
bands like Nirvana, Hole, Smashing Pumpkins, Blind
Melon, Red Hot Chili Peppers, Stone Temple Pilots, Alice in
Chains Sex Pistols, Porno for Pyros and Depeche Mode—to
name just a few. These bands and others like them have
sold over sixty million albums to middle-class teenagers
across the nation. Talk about a spiritual vacuum in our
country and the failure of the public school system.
Ordinary middle-class parents raise their children with no
values or spiritual beliefs, and their kids end up worshiping
rock stars who are junkies.

Even the fashion industry is reeling from the impact of
this explosion of heroin use. A new fashion look called
"heroin chique" is now the rage. Models who look
wasted or who look as if they are addicted to heroin are
the "in" thing. U.S. heroin production has doubled since
the mid-1980s. The use of other drugs like crack, marijuana,
cocaine, hallucinogens, stimulants and tranquilizers is
going through the roof. Only fasting, prayer and revival
can save this generation from being destroyed by the
demonic power behind these drugs.

According to the Drug Enforcement Administration
(DEA), 62 percent of all the heroin seized in the United
States is coming from Colombia. Colombia is the major

exporter of cocaine in the United States as well. What is even more disturbing is the recent allegations that our own CIA was involved in the selling of drugs in inner cities of America such as Los Angeles in order to finance a covert war in Nicaragua.

A new drug called gamma hydroxybutyrate (GHB) is the nation's hottest party drug. Unfortunately it can cause death. A fifteen-year-old named Lucas Bielat gulped down this drug in the California desert and began frothing up blood and died.[1] Across the nation at what are called "rave scenes," young people are abusing drugs like GHB, Rohypnol and Ecstasy.

The Book of Revelation teaches us that in the last days drug use will be widespread and common. Drug use, immorality and spiritual deception go hand in hand. Satan uses drugs as a powerful weapon to ensnare mankind.

SATANISM AND OUR YOUTH

One of the symptoms of how far our nation has strayed is the fact that growing numbers of our young people are beginning to experiment with things like Satanism and the occult. For years now, satanic symbols have adorned the covers of rock 'n roll albums, and many of the largest rock bands in the world openly proclaim their involvement in Satanism. However, the real nature of Satanism is beginning to rear its ugly head. In San Luis Obisbo, California, three middle-class teenaged boys drugged, raped and murdered a fifteen-year-old girl as part of a satanic ritual.

The teenage boys believed that the murder of a virgin on

Satan's altar would earn them a ticket to hell. When the news media showed the three teenage boys coming out of the court room, these young men looked like ordinary teenagers, the kind you might see living next door to your house. Yet, they had become Satanists and savagely murdered a young teenage girl. The alarming thing is that satanic involvement is growing among teenagers. The recent interest in the movie *The Blair Witch Project* reflects this new national obsession among young people with witchcraft, Satanism and the occult.

In West Memphis, Arkansas, three eight-year-old boys were murdered in a grisly ritualistic sacrifice by three teenaged boys who were into heavy metal music and Satanism. In fact, all across the nation reports are coming in about animal and human sacrifices and the rise of satanic cults. Some of the more sensational stories involve people like David Ramirez, the "Night Stalker" who boldly declared "Hail Satan" on the televised proceedings in a court room.

An entire generation has been raised in an atmosphere devoid of moral absolutes and is open to seduction from the dark spiritual forces that energize satanic cults. Just the other day I walked into a convenience store where I was waited on by a young man in his late teens or early twenties. He had very long hair tied in a pony tail. I noticed that a very large silver medallion hung from a chain around his neck. As I observed the medallion more closely, I recognized that it was in the shape of a pentagram, which is a symbol of Satan worship. It sent chills down my spine to think about what this young man might be into. I prayed for him silently and asked Jesus Christ to save him and deliver him from darkness. I took up my responsibility as an intercessor and bound the powers of darkness operating in his life. In addition, I prayed for the safety of the community and that any group of Satan worshipers in that area would be rendered inoperative.

If you think this is some kind of isolated incident, then think again. As I have spoken across this nation on the subject of Bible prophecy, the New Age and the occult, I have been told many times by the people attending the conferences that young people in those communities are involved in Satanism and witchcraft.

SUMMING IT UP: WHAT DOES IT ALL MEAN?

I was a guest on the international *Art Bell Show* for two hours. During the course of the interview, Art Bell asked me about what he terms "earth changes"—the increases in freak weather, earthquakes and other cataclysmic changes happening on our planet. Unlike many in the media, Art understands the significance of the major changes that are happening on our planet.

We are in a time like no other time before us. Due to nuclear and biological technology, mankind now has the capacity to eradicate totally all life forms from Planet Earth. Never before in the history of the world has the potential to destroy the entire earth been placed in the hands of so many people. Rogue nations like Iran and North Korea now have the capacity to throw the entire world into World War III and to release atomic weapons that can bring on the horrible devastation of what scientists call a "nuclear winter."[2]

Terrorists from militant Islamic countries can secretly bring in biological or nuclear weapons and make what happened in Oklahoma City look like a Sunday school picnic. In addition, the extent of violent crime in a so-called civilized nation like the United States is unprecedented in modern times. Even Nazi Germany with all of its horrors did not have serial killers, child molesters, drive-by shootings and the other crimes that plague our nation. Where in the history of mankind do we see things like the student massacre at Columbine High School and other school shootings? The answer is never! Never before in the history of civilization do we see the kind of evil and moral anarchy that we see now.

Sodom and Gomorrah had degenerated into this kind of moral anarchy, and they were supernaturally destroyed by God in judgment. In the days of Noah right before the flood, the Book of Genesis indicates that the entire earth had become filled with violence and wickedness. In both of these cases, the people had become so corrupt and depraved that God sent divine judgment.

Here in our own nation we are experiencing an unprecedented increase in destructive earthquakes, tornadoes, hurricanes, floods, droughts and heat waves. Record hot and cold temperatures are being set all over the nation. Yet, as a people we fail to discern as our ancestors did the relationship between these natural disasters and our spiritual condition as a nation.

Even the Indians understood that there was a direct relationship between destructive natural forces and spirituality. In fact, most ancient peoples, no matter how pagan, understood that nature and spirituality are connected. The ancient Jews were well aware of the fact that their relationship with God was connected to things like the weather, the condition of their crops, military victory and so on. In the Old Testament, God spelled out to the Israelites the numerous blessings that would be theirs if they would "diligently obey the voice of the LORD [their] God, to observe carefully all His commandments" (Deut. 28:1). In addition, they understood that if they violated God's laws and followed after other gods, they would be cursed.

Here in America, which was once a Judeo-Christian nation, we have turned our backs on God and have followed after the gods of money, power, sex and materialism. In our unbelievable pride and arrogance, we look at the increase of natural disasters and the breakdown of society as due to things like global warming and a lack of self-esteem. How pathetically foolish and blind we have become as a people.

Without a doubt there is a relationship between our spiritual condition—the fact that as a nation we have turned our backs on God—and the curses we see unleashed upon our land. Our wholesale rejection of God in favor of humanism and New Age beliefs, our slaughter of a million unborn babies a year, our legitimizing of homosexual marriages and perversion and our greed and materialism have caused a protective spiritual covering by a loving God to be removed, and we are reaping what we have sown. We have sown to the wind, and we are now reaping a whirlwind of destruction and upheaval.

In a sense we have opened Pandora's box, and there seems to be no turning back. Everything from hard-core pornographic images of bestiality, homosexuality, sadism and perversion on the Internet to the ultra-violence in our streets indicates that there is something very wrong with America. America was founded as a Christian nation blessed by God, and it has turned into a pagan nation that worships false gods.

Our planet is on the verge of entering what the Bible calls the "Great Tribulation." The only thing holding back the full onslaught of evil in our world today is the fact that the church is still here. When this restraining force is removed, I believe literally that all hell will break loose.

MARILYN MANSON, ANTICHRIST SUPERSTAR

What is happening in popular culture is symptomatic of just how pervasive the tide of immorality is in our nation and world. A lot of people are in total denial as to just how bad things really are. A case in point would be the popularity of rock superstar Marilyn Manson, who just happens to be a guy. Manson's best-selling album, *Antichrist Superstar*, glorifies a lifestyle of Satanism, drugs, sexual perversion and the occult. Dressed up looking like a cross between a vampire and a transvestite, Marilyn Manson was educated in a fundamentalist Christian elementary school.

75

In his autobiography, *The Long Road Out of Hell*, Manson tells of the time that he and his band covered a deaf groupie with luncheon meat, and then proceeded to give her a "golden shower" (urinate on her). There are many other things that Manson and his band do that are simply too decadent and evil for me to present in this book. But the most terrifying thing is that he is the idol of millions of teenagers around the world!

Another contemporary rock group called Blink 182, from San Diego, sings about incest, masturbation and bestiality. Many rap groups sing about killing cops and raping and sodomizing women. Perversion, decadence, Satanism, suicide and the occult are common themes in today's music scene. I remember when as a feature-film producer I met rock star Alice Cooper at his agent's home in Bel Air. Alice (also a he) was one of the first rock stars to wear makeup and dress up like a Halloween character. But by today's standards Alice Cooper comes off like a Sunday school teacher!

On every front in our society, evil and wickedness are being paraded and glorified with hardly a hint of protest. Shock-radio jock Howard Stern entertains tens of millions of Americans on their way to work each morning with lewd jokes and pornographic humor. During the morning, with young children watching, television host Jerry Springer features shows like a girl having sex with over a hundred men in the making of a pornographic movie. The Brooklyn Museum of Art in New York opened a show called "Sensation." The exhibit featured elephant dung and cutouts of women's behinds, Larry Flynt-style, over the Virgin Mary.³

Authors like Charles Gatewood write books like *True Blood,* which show explicit photographs of those who engage in the newest form of decadence called "blood play," where men and women have sex while covered in their own blood, spilt by self-inflicted cuts. Our universities feature courses on homosexual sex, sado-masochism and the occult. One major Southern California university offered an "art class," featuring an ex-female porn star engaged in sex acts with two other women in the class! Yet, the silence of the lack of moral outrage across our nation is deafening!

Across the wide spectrum of our global society we are seeing the floodgates of hell pouring out sexual perversion, cruelty, wickedness, degradation, violence and greed of every kind. Child prostitution, murder, incest, torture and ultra-violent crimes are escalating to a dizzying degree.

A FINAL MANIFESTATION OF EVIL

What many people do not understand is that this final manifestation of the evil that exists in the heart of sinful man is a prophetic sign that this entire planet is about to enter the most horrible period of all history. As bad as things are, there is still a force on the earth holding back the full tide of evil from sweeping this earth. This restraining force is called the church, and when the church is removed by the Rapture, all hell is going to break loose.

I believe America and the world has entered the slippery

slope of judgment. At some point known only to God, our planet will be plunged into the Great Tribulation. But before that time a powerful, charismatic world leader will emerge to seduce the nations and the people with a false message of hope, peace and prosperity. The world is eager to follow a leader who can offer peace and prosperity, even if this leader is the Antichrist himself.

History repeats itself, and modern history shows us how easily a Lenin, Stalin, Mao, Hitler and Castro can come to power promising false hope. The untold millions who were murdered under the regimes of these men, and the unspeakable oppression that followed, should testify to the dangers inherent in the absolute power of the State. But right here in America the same danger lurks in the shadows. Very slowly our rights and religious frcedoms are being taken from us without most people even realizing it.

This time it is different, because never before in the world's history has government had the technological power to exercise total control of people through computers, satellites, microchip implants, television cameras and digital cash. In addition, with the advent of a global economy, the mass media and unprecedented military power, a supranational state under the leadership of a world leader can emerge to unify the nations.

What we are seeing in our generation is a massive convergence of prophetic signs. Although no one can predict for sure how close we are to things like the Rapture of the church or the Second Coming of Jesus Christ, it is clear that the "signs of the times" of which Jesus Christ spoke in

Matthew 24 indicate that we are drawing closer to the fulfillment of biblical prophecy. Many people have discredited Bible prophecy by foolish speculation and the attempt to assign specific dates. The purpose of this book is not to set times or make predictions. It is simply to help us become the kind of people that God wants us to be and to do the things He has assigned us to do.

THE ARMAGEDDON CLOCK IS COUNTING DOWN

The Bible has much to say regarding the end of the age. Throughout the Old and New Testaments we are given powerful prophecies to enlighten us about the significant times in which we live. These prophecies are filled with words of admonition, warning, encouragement and revelation to the nations of the earth. Let's take a closer look at the nations and the events preceding Armageddon in light of Bible prophecy. It will not take long to realize that the biblical prophecies are falling into place rapidly. Each event is like another tick on the Armageddon clock, bringing us ever nearer to Christ's return.

Section II
What Does the Bible Say?

Seventy weeks are determined . . .

—DANIEL 9:24

....

10

Quantum Shift

M OST PEOPLE TODAY have absolutely no idea what is going to happen to our world in the next few years. Like people in some quiet Pennsylvania Dutch community who choose to ride in wagons and forego modern technology, yet suddenly see a 747 jet roar above their heads or a high-speed Mercedes speed by them on the road, our world is about to be shattered by the quantum shift that is coming.

All of the seemingly separate forces such as global economics, technology, political upheaval and sociological forces are now merging to produce a quantum shift in the way life is lived on our planet. The seeds of change that were quietly sowed in the 1950s are starting to come to maturity all around us.

We are going to see nothing less than a horrific merger of these forces, eventually catapulting us into the Great Tribulation. These seemingly separate streams of occurrence, appearing to happen randomly, are going to collide into a kind of cosmic explosion and a revolution in the way we live.

In the near future we can expect the following:

- A merger of occultic/supernatural forces with political governments
- A merger of technology with occult powers
- Additional massive global weather changes
- A complete takeover of the educational system by humanistic forces that will attack Christian beliefs
- A major military move with Russia, Iran and their allies against Israel
- A cashless society
- Artificially intelligent computers with consciousness

SEVENTY WEEKS OF DANIEL

In Daniel 9:24–27 we are introduced to the "Seventy

Weeks of Daniel," a precise prophetic timeline of what is going to happen in our world prophetically. The time frame of seventy weeks or "seventy sevens of years" has to do with Daniel's people, the Jews.

> Seventy weeks are determined
> For your people and for your
>   holy city,
> To finish the transgression,
> To make an end of sins,
> To make reconciliation for
>   iniquity,
> To bring in everlasting
>   righteousness,
> To seal up vision and prophecy,
> And to anoint the Most Holy.
>
> Know therefore and under-
>   stand,
> That from the going forth of
>   the command
> To restore and build Jerusalem
> Until Messiah the Prince,
> There shall be seven weeks and
>   sixty-two weeks;
> The street shall be built again,
>   and the wall,
> Even in troublesome times.
>
> And after the sixty-two weeks
> Messiah shall be cut off, but not

> for Himself;
> And the people of the prince
>   who is to come
> Shall destroy the city and the
>   sanctuary.
> The end of it shall be with a
>   flood,
> And till the end of the war
>   desolations are determined.
> Then he shall confirm a
>   covenant with many for one
>   week;
> But in the middle of the
>   week
> He shall bring an end to
>   sacrifice and offering.
> And on the wing of
>   abominations shall be one
>   who makes desolate,
> Even until the consummation,
>   which is determined,
> Is poured out on the desolate.
>
> —DANIEL 9:24–27

DECIPHERING DANIEL'S MESSAGE

In reading this portion of Daniel it is important to understand a number of key facts. First of all, the seventy weeks are 490 years composed of 360-day years. The Jewish calendar was based on a biblical lunar-solar year of 360 days. Our current calendar is based on a solar year of 365.25 days. The fact that the weeks of years were based on 360-day years can be confirmed by comparing Daniel 7:25; Revelation 11:2–3; 12:6, 14; and 13:5.

The weeks of years began with a command by Artaxerxes in 445 B.C. to rebuild Jerusalem. From 445 B.C. to 396 B.C. we have seven sevens, or forty-nine years. This covers Artaxerxes' decree up to the time of Nehemiah and the covenant renewal celebration in Jerusalem.

In Daniel 9:25 we read, "There shall be seven weeks and sixty-two weeks," or seven sevens and sixty-two sevens. The sixty-two sevens equal 434 years, or 396 B.C. to A.D. 32. This time period of sixty-two sevens begins with the dedication of the second temple and continues to the crucifixion of our Lord Jesus Christ. This leaves one seven, or seven years, that are yet unfulfilled. This last seven-year period is known as "the time of Jacob's trouble," or the Tribulation.

The seventy weeks of Daniel speak of a total of seventy sevens or seventy weeks of years, which total 490 years. This began with Artaxerxes' command to rebuild the walls of Jerusalem on March 14, 445 B.C. until the time when Messiah was to be "cut off," which was April 6, A.D. 32.

The seventy weeks of Daniel outline a precise prophetic timetable of what is going to happen in the last days. First we have seven weeks, or 49 years, which lasted from 445 B.C. to 396 B.C. Then a time period known as "sixty-two sevens," or 62 weeks, began, which is 434 years. This time period ended in A.D. 32 when the Messiah was "cut off"— Jesus Christ was crucified. After

A.D. 32 there is a gap between the sixty-two weeks and the final seventieth week. We have not yet ended the seventieth week of Daniel. Many Bible scholars believe that this seventieth week of Daniel will begin when the church of Jesus Christ is raptured from the earth and the Antichrist is then revealed.

In a sense, God's prophetic clock stopped on A.D. 32 when Israel rejected their Messiah. From that time on we have entered into what is called the Church Age. The Church Age will cease when the church is raptured from the earth, and the seventieth week of Daniel will then begin.

UNDERSTANDING CURRENT EVENTS

Although no one knows the date of Christ's return, the timing of the Rapture or at what exact time the seventieth week of Daniel will begin, if we study our Bible carefully, we can understand current events. The Bible is the most exciting book ever written, and it is completely relevant to what is happening today. Although many of our world leaders and military and intelligence services seem to be in the dark as to what is going on in our world, a serious student of the Bible will have the ability to understand global economic, political and social trends.

Many people have attempted to "spiritualize" the Bible, turning the messages of books like Ezekiel, Daniel and Revelation into allegorical books. But these books speak in precise detail of what is happening today on a global level. The rise of faces in Russia, the explosive economic and military growth of China, the reality of Iran's role in exporting terrorism, the coming cashless society, the push toward one world government, a United Europe, the Middle East peace process and other trends are predicted in the Bible.

In addition, the increase in earthquakes, disease outbreaks and the social disintegration of our society were predicted around two thousand years ago by Jesus Christ. Although there are countless intelligence gathering agencies, corporations like the Rand Corporation and groups like the World Future Society, none of these groups seem to take the Bible seriously. As such, they are unable to predict accurately the future of mankind.

The Bible is not just some book of fairy tales on the same level as Mother Goose. Nor is it a book of myths, as writer Joseph Campbell would suggest. In his arrogance, modern man has dismissed the fact that the Bible has supernatural authorship and speaks quite profoundly about science, history, culture, medicine, biology, society and man's future.

The Middle East's role is at the heart of End-Time events. Let's find out why.

Abraham had two sons, one by the bondwoman and one by the free woman. But the son by the bondwoman was born according to the flesh, and the son by the free woman through the promise.

—GALATIANS 4:22–23, NAS

11

The Origins
of the Conflict

I N LOOKING AT the current situation in the Middle East, it is crucial that we understand the real source of the conflict between the Muslim world and Israel. The roots of this conflict go back to the time of Abraham when God promised to bless Abraham with an heir. Abraham and Sarah were getting on in years, and they began to doubt God's promise of a child. Sarah came up with the idea that Abraham should have sexual relations with her maidservant, Hagar.

This was not a good idea, and Sarah regretted allowing her husband to impregnate Hagar. Soon after Hagar realized she was pregnant, Hagar began to hate Sarah, and Sarah began to treat her very poorly. Hagar had a son by Abraham called Ishmael. Around fourteen years after Ishmael was born, Sarah and Abraham had a son called Isaac, who was born of God's promise.

The Bible teaches us that there was a conflict between Ishmael and Isaac from the very beginning of their relationship. Genesis 21:9 says, "And Sarah saw the son of Hagar the Egyptian, whom she had borne to Abraham, scoffing." Ishmael's behavior toward Isaac bothered Sarah greatly. The Hebrew word for *scoffing* means "playing, teasing or reproaching." The apostle Paul used the word *persecuted* in describing Ishmael's treatment of Isaac (Gal. 4:29).

Isaac was the child of God's promise. Ishmael had been "born according to the flesh"; Isaac was "born according to the promise" (v. 29).

God loved Hagar and Ishmael as well as Abraham, Sarah and Isaac. Even though Ishmael was not the child of God's promise, God still had enormous compassion and love for Ishmael. In Genesis 21:17–18 we read, "And God heard the voice of the lad. Then the angel of God called to Hagar out of heaven, and said to her, 'What ails you, Hagar? Fear not, for God has heard the voice of the lad where he is. Arise, lift up the lad and hold him with your hand, for I will make him a great nation.'"

God promised that Ishmael's descendants would make a great nation. Ishmael had twelve sons who became twelve princes and settled the Arabian Peninsula. Many Bible scholars believe that Egyptians, Midianites, Edomites, Assyrians and other groups came from Ishmael. Islamic belief also teaches that Ishmael was the father of the desert peoples of the Middle East.

Today's Muslims have as their great ancestor Ishmael. Historically, beginning with their father, Ishmael, these groups have been jealous over Isaac and his descendants —the modern children of Israel. Islam even teaches that Jews rewrote the Bible to teach that it was only the Jews who were heirs to the Abrahamic covenant, which stipulates that the land of Israel belongs to the Jews. Islamic teachers teach that Abraham had eight sons, not just two. They say that it was Ishmael and not Isaac whom Abraham almost sacrificed on Mount Moriah. The Koran teaches that the Abrahamic covenant, along with the promise of the land of Israel, was given to the Arabs through Ishmael.

However, the Bible clearly teaches that Israel was given to the Jews who were the descendants of Isaac. Genesis 17:19–21 states:

> Then God said: "No, Sarah your wife shall bear you a son, and you shall call his name Isaac; I will establish My covenant with him for an everlasting covenant, and with his descendants after him. And as for Ishmael, I have heard you. Behold, I have blessed him, and will make him fruitful, and will multiply him exceedingly. He shall beget twelve princes, and I will make him a great nation. But My covenant I will establish with Isaac, whom Sarah shall bear to you at this same time next year."

As we have already seen, Ishmael had twelve sons who became the twelve princes prophesied in Genesis 17:20. But the promise of the Abrahamic covenant, which included the title deed to Israel, was made specifically to Isaac and his descendants.

At the very root of the current Middle East conflict lies this ancient jealousy that Ishmael had toward Isaac over four thousand years ago. The problems in the Middle East are spiritual in origin, and peace negotiations that are based solely on geography and economics are doomed to failure. God loves the Muslim and the Arab, and He sent Jesus Christ to die for them, just as He did for you and me. But there are many problems with the fundamental teachings of Islam and the Koran. The Bible states quite clearly that the Abrahamic covenant was given to Isaac and descendants and not to the descendants of Ishmael.

In short, the Jews have a real estate deed from God on the land of Israel. The world's refusal to acknowledge that fact is rooted in its rejection of the reality of God's existence and a denial of the authority of God's Word. The problems in the Middle East will lead to the ultimate humanistic solution—the acceptance of the Antichrist—even by the Jews. This will lead to a betrayal of the Jews by the Antichrist, Armageddon and the Second Coming of Jesus Christ.

WHAT A REAL ESTATE DEAL

Now the LORD had said to Abram: "Get out of your country, from your family and from your father's

94

house, to a land that I will show you. I will make you a great nation; I will bless you and make your name great…I will bless those who bless you, and I will curse him who curses you."

—GENESIS 12:1–3

In understanding the current conflict in the Middle East, it is important to understand who actually owns the land. If we read the original biblical account, we see that God gave Israel the land to possess forever and ever. Jeremiah 7:7 says, "Then I will cause you to dwell in this place, in the land that I gave to your fathers forever and ever." Genesis 15:18 says, "On the same day the LORD made a covenant with Abram, saying: 'To your descendants I have given this land, from the river of Egypt to the great river, the River Euphrates.'"

The Bible is quite clear that God gave the land of Israel to Abraham's descendants, who are the children of Israel. In Genesis 28:13 we read, "And behold, the LORD stood above it and said: 'I am the LORD God of Abraham your father and the God of Isaac; the land on which you lie I will give to you and your descendants.'" God repeats this theme when talking to Isaac many times. Genesis 26:2–3 says, "Then the LORD appeared to him and said: 'Do not go down to Egypt; live in the land of which I tell you. Dwell in this land, and I will be with you and bless you; for to you and your descendants I will give all these lands, and I will perform the oath which I swore to Abraham your father.'"

God's promise to give Israel the land is repeated throughout the Old Testament. God says in Exodus 6:8, "And I will bring you into the land which I swore to give Abraham, Isaac, and Jacob; and I will give it to you as a heritage: I am the LORD." In Leviticus 20:24, God says again, "But I have said to you, 'You shall inherit their land, and I will give it to you to possess, a land flowing with milk and honey.' I am the LORD your God, who has separated you from the peoples."

Although there is great debate among Jews, Muslims, Christians and political leaders as to who actually owns the land, it is clear from the Bible that God made a contractual promise or covenant to give the nation of Israel this most desirous piece of real estate.

The United States government, along with the globalist community, has consistently pressured Israel to give up land in order to maintain peace. The Clinton Administration has been pressuring Ehud Barak to give an additional 13 percent of the West Bank to the Palestinians. In fact, many of the so-called peace efforts revolve around Israel making concessions and giving up land.

Israel plans to expand Jewish settlements in the Golan Heights. Israel captured the Golan Heights in the 1967 Six-Day War and has settled over 15,000 Jews in the area. The new plan calls for 2,300 housing units and 2,500 holiday apartments overlooking the Sea of Galilee. Syria is in strong opposition to this move, and there is a tremendous conflict going on over this plan. Yet God gave Israel this land.

Jesus also indicated that Israel's vital role in End-Time

events would signal the rest of the world regarding the timing of Jesus' return.

THE SIGN OF THE FIG TREE

> Then He spoke to them in a parable: "Look at the fig tree, and all the trees. When they are already budding, you see and know for yourselves that summer is now near. So you also, when you see these things happening, know that the kingdom of God is near. Assuredly, I say to you, this generation will by no means pass away till all these things take place. Heaven and earth will pass away, but My words will by no means pass away."
>
> —LUKE 21:29–33

Jesus Christ used the parable of the fig tree to illustrate the time when He would return to earth to set up His kingdom. The fig tree represents the nation of Israel. For over nineteen hundred years the Jews were dispersed around the world until Israel was reformed as a nation in 1948. The physical return of the Jews to Israel and the reformation of the nation of Israel represents the fig tree. The exodus of Jews around the world to return to their homeland represents the budding of the fig tree.

Jeremiah 24:5–7 says:

> Thus says the Lord, the God of Israel: "Like these good figs, so I will acknowledge those who are carried away captive from Judah, whom I have sent out of this place for their own good, into the land of the

> Chaldeans. For I will set My eyes for them for good, and I will bring them back to this land; I will build them and not pull them down, and I will plant them and not pluck them up. Then I will give them a heart to know Me, that I am the Lord; and they shall be My people, and I will be their God, for they shall return to Me with their whole heart."

The Bible prophesies that in the last days the Jews who were dispersed will be returned to Jerusalem. Then some time after their physical return, the Jews are prophesied to return to their Messiah, Jesus Christ, which would represent the fig tree bearing fruit and blossoming.

In Ezekiel 37:1–28 we see Ezekiel prophesying to dead bones that represent a spiritually dead nation of Israel. But the Spirit of the Lord breathes upon them, and they come alive. "So I prophesied as He commanded me, and breath came into them, and they lived, and stood upon their feet, an exceedingly great army" (Ezek. 37:10).

This represents an End-Time spiritual restoration of the nation of Israel. Chapter 37 of Ezekiel prophesies a *physical* return of the Jews from all the nations of the earth, and then a *spiritual* rebirth. In Ezekiel 36 we read also about the Jews being gathered from all the nations of the earth for a return to their own land (v. 24). Ezekiel 37:11 speaks about a physical restoration of national Israel (coming together as the whole house of Israel).

Then in Ezekiel 37:8, Ezekiel speaks of a spiritual revival. Thirty years ago there were only about fifty to one hundred Jewish believers in Jesus Christ living in Israel. Today there are about six to seven thousand Jews who have accepted Jesus Christ as their Lord and Savior in Israel with about seventy to eighty Messianic congregations where Jews unite to worship Jesus Christ. Truly the fig tree is about to blossom, which means that Jesus Christ is at the door and ready to return. When spiritual revival begins to spread in Israel, then we will see a fulfillment of Luke 21:29–33. The election of Ehud Barak as Prime Minister of Israel has prophetic significance. Many of the conservative and liberal Jews in Israel have grown weary of the control of Israel by the orthodox community. In addition, the orthodox community has siphoned off government funds in order to finance their own agendas.

The defeat of Netanyahu represents an overthrow of orthodox control. It has been the orthodox community that militantly persecuted Jews who accepted Jesus Christ as their Messiah. The election of Ehud Barak represents a loosening of orthodoxy's grip and the beginning of a spiritual climate that will allow for the further spread of the gospel of Jesus Christ among Jews in Israel.[1]

EHUD BARAK, PRIME MINISTER OF ISRAEL

With the help of the Clinton Administration, Ehud Barak was elected as Prime Minister of Israel. Bill Clinton even sent in the "raging Cajun," James Carville, to assure Barak's election. Clearly, the global establishment wanted a more moderate head of Israel—one who would play ball with the Palestinians, the globalists and the U.S. government.

At a meeting in Penha Longa Resort in Sinatra, Portugal, the Bilderbergers met to discuss the Kosovo war, the replacement of NATO with a Western European army and the fate of Israel. The Bilderbergers are preparing for a Middle East peace settlement and the final declaration of a Palestinian State. They will also help decide the fate of Jerusalem and of the Golan Heights. The election of Ehud Barak was pivotal in the globalist strategy.

Ehud Barak has already gone on record stating that he is in favor of Israel's not giving up the Golan Heights as part of the peace process. Also, Ehud Barak has close ties to the Clinton Administration and is not willing to give up land for peace in Israel.

Therefore when you see the "abomination of desolation," spoken of by Daniel the prophet, standing in the holy place (whoever reads, let him understand) . . .

—MATTHEW 24:15

12

The Antichrist

A FTER THE NATION of Israel is regathered and the fig tree has budded, events will continue to unfold in Israel. A wicked ruler will rise up in God's nation.

Immediately after the passages of scripture outlining the signs of the times in Matthew 24, Jesus Christ gave the warning about the abomination of desolation. He was referring to what the prophet Daniel had spoken about in Daniel 9:27:

> Then he shall confirm a covenant with many for one week; but in the middle of the week he shall bring an end to sacrifice and offering. And on the wing of abominations shall be one who makes desolate, even

until the consummation, which is determined, is poured out on the desolate.

What this passage of scripture is talking about is a future time when the nation of Israel will enter into a covenant or peace treaty with the Antichrist. The Antichrist is the one to whom Jesus Christ was referring in Matthew 24:15 when He used the term "abomination of desolation." In 168 B.C., the Syrian ruler Antiochus Epiphanes destroyed the Jewish temple and set up his own image in the temple to be worshiped. This was a foreshadowing of what would happen in the last days, when the Antichrist will set himself up in the temple to be worshiped as God. That will be the *abomination of desolation.*

In 2 Thessalonians 2:3–4 the apostle Paul says:

Let no one deceive you by any means; for that Day will not come unless the falling away comes first, and the man of sin is revealed, the son of perdition, who opposes and exalts himself above all that is called God or that is worshiped, so that he sits as God in the temple of God, showing himself that he is God.

The time is coming when a powerful charismatic world leader, whom the Bible calls the Antichrist, is going to emerge on the world scene and set himself up in the Jewish temple demanding to be worshiped as God.

Will this abomination of desolation be the Antichrist himself or some kind of virtual reality image generated by technology? Perhaps this image will be a 3-D holograph that will be set up in the temple. Only time will reveal exactly who or what this abomination of desolation will be. But one thing will be for sure—it will usher in the return of Christ.

THE BEAST OUT OF THE SEA

> Then I stood on the sand of the sea. And I saw a beast rising up out of the sea, having seven heads and ten horns, and on his horns ten crowns, and on his heads a blasphemous name. Now the beast which I saw was like a leopard, his feet were like the feet of a bear, and his mouth like the mouth of a lion. The dragon gave him his power, his throne, and great authority.
>
> —REVELATION 13:1–2

This passage of scripture speaks of a coming world ruler of a revived Roman Empire. This description is similar to Daniel 7:7–8, Revelation 12:3 and 17:3, 7. These verses tell us two very interesting things about this future world dictator: First, he will get his power directly from Satan, or the "dragon." Second, this leader rises out of the sea, the great mass of humanity that represents the Gentile powers of the world.

This beast is compared to a leopard with the feet of a bear and the mouth of a lion. This comparison of the beast to these animals is similar to Daniel 7, where the successive world empires are represented by the lion, which symbolized Babylon; the bear, which was the Medo-Persian empire; and the leopard, which represented the Alexandrian Empire. The fourth empire contains all these elements, and it will be this revived Roman Empire that will be ruled by the Antichrist during the Great Tribulation.

BEAST NUMBER TWO

> Then I saw another beast coming up out of the earth, and he had two horns like a lamb and spoke like a dragon. And he exercises all authority of the first beast in his presence, and causes those who dwell in it to worship the first beast, whose deadly wound was healed. He performs great signs, so that he even makes fire come down from heaven on the earth in the sight of men.
>
> —REVELATION 13:11–13

The Bible very clearly states that there will be more than one beast. In addition to the Antichrist there will come this second beast, or the false prophet. The very fact that this false prophet has "two horns like a lamb" indicates that he has a religious character. He will masquerade as a loving spiritual prophet, but he "spoke like a dragon" (Rev. 13:11).

In other words, the false prophet will also be energized supernaturally by Satan. The false prophet will be the head of some kind of End-Times religious system. In fact, the false prophet may head up an apostate church. His role will be to cause people to worship the Antichrist, and he will have great supernatural power. In Revelation 13:13 it says, "He performs great signs, so that he even makes fire come down from heaven on the earth in the sight of men."

This false prophet may call down a supernatural display

of fire from outer space that will astound the whole world. With the recent rise of interest in UFO phenomena and the subject of aliens from outer space, it is possible that this "New Age" religion of the false prophet may incorporate beliefs about extraterrestrial visitors from other planets. Many people in our nation now believe that the United States government has conspired in some kind of massive cover-up about alien encounters in our world. In addition, there are growing numbers of people who claim to have had firsthand direct encounters with aliens.

Personally, I think the majority of these claims are the result of wishful imaginations, fantasy and involvement with the occult. However, I do think that there is a significant percentage of people who have had real supernatural experiences with what they believe are aliens. In other words, I think these people have experienced some kind of visitation. But I believe that these aliens are not visitors from other planets. I think that they are visitors from another dimension of the invisible realm. In short, it is my opinion that these people are actually having encounters with demons.

People like best-selling author Whitley Streiber, who wrote of his encounters with aliens in books like *Transformation: The Breakthrough,* have had significant involvement with the occult before having these encounter experiences.[1] I think what they are experiencing is demonic activity—not alien activity. There is a remarkable similarity to the description of what these aliens look like and what some people describe demons to look like.

In any case, when the Bible says that the false prophet makes fire come down from the sky, it may be alluding to a supernatural display of power or to some kind of demonstration by aliens who are, in reality, demons.

THE MARK OF THE BEAST

> He causes all, both small and great, rich and poor, free and slave, to receive a mark on their right hand or on their foreheads, and that no one may buy or sell except one who has the mark or the name of the beast, or the number of his name. Here is wisdom. Let him who has understanding calculate the number of the beast, for it is the number of a man: His number is 666.
>
> —REVELATION 13:16–18

I remember growing up and going to the local super-market to buy groceries. Usually you paid in cash. A number of years later, they took checks if they knew you. Now in just a matter of a few years, ATM machines have been put in all the supermarkets, and you can pay with your ATM card or any major credit card. The entire system has been revolutionized in just a few years! But that's just the beginning of the revolution. Our society is going cashless—cash will soon become obsolete. Instead you will pay for everything with credit cards or comput-erized smart cards.

Using technology straight out of the movie *Mission Impossible,* ATMs worldwide are now being tested with a new electronic device that will identify consumers by taking an electronic photo of their eye when they walk up to an ATM machine. A Moorestown, New Jersey, company called Sensar has invented an ID system that takes pictures of a customer's iris. Citibank has spent more than $3 million to help invent this technology, because they believe that PIN numbers are often lost or stolen.[2]

The Bible tells us that the time will come when the world will operate under a single economic system that will be headed up by the Antichrist. In this system no one will be able to buy or sell without a mark on your right hand or forehead. This will be what the Bible calls the "mark of the beast," or the 666 system. In actuality, it is the false prophet who will set up the 666 economic system.

A number of years ago it seemed impossible that a world dictator could set up a "mark of the beast" system that would control all financial transactions. For many years people thought that it would be some kind of tattoo on the right hand or forehead. But now, secular financial analysts are telling us that they are planning to use a computerized microchip implant in the hand or possibly the forehead within the decade. Although there is not necessarily anything evil about this technology itself, it certainly outlines a scenario where a 666 system could be put in place overnight.

This system could become evil or an instrument of the Antichrist when the condition for receiving such an implant on your hand or forehead was a requirement to renounce your faith in Jesus Christ and worship the Antichrist. There is nothing evil about credit cards, computerized smart cards and possibly even microchip implants—until they become part of the Antichrist system. However, I know many Christians who are going to refuse any kind of microchip implant, because they feel it will immediately lead to the "mark of the beast."

The Book of Revelation states that when this Antichrist system is in place, people will be forced to worship the "image of the beast" or be killed. "He was granted power to give breath to the image of the beast, that the image of the beast should both speak and cause as many as would not worship the image of the beast to be killed" (Rev. 13:15).

When one decides to take the "mark of the beast," that person is making a decision to renounce Jesus Christ as Lord and actually worship the Antichrist—Satan's representative—as god. The Bible says that there will be a very heavy price to pay for those who do so. In fact, during this time God is going to send an angel to warn people against doing such a thing:

> Then a third angel followed them, saying with a loud voice, "If anyone worships the beast and his image, and receives his mark on his forehead or on his hand, he himself shall also drink of the wine of the wrath of God, which is poured out full strength into the cup of His indignation. He shall be tormented with fire and brimstone in the presence of the holy angels and in the presence of the Lamb."
> —REVELATION 14:9–10

According to God, taking the mark of the beast is serious business. Revelation 14:11 says, "And the smoke of their torment ascends forever and ever; and they have no rest day or night, who worship the beast and his image, and whoever receives the mark of his name."

Mark of the Beast Technology?

There is a whole new generation of biotechnology that looks as if it were lifted right out of the pages of the Book of Revelation. This new technology of biochip implants can place a tiny computer chip inside the skin of a human being or animal for identification or tracking purposes. Japan has just invested over $250 million in a ten-year program to develop a whole new system of bio-implants.[3]

Basically, this new biochip technology consists of passive or active bio-implants. A passive bio-implant is something like an ATM card strip, in that it can be scanned and then deliver certain information such as name, address, social security number and health information. The other kind of bio-implant has its own internal electronics, which can send out an electronic signal.

The Destron IDI bio-implant is the size of a grain of rice and has an electromagnetic barcode in it. It is encapsulated in inert material and is biocompatible so that it won't trigger an antigen reaction when it is placed inside a body. This device is basically used on animals in order to prevent theft or loss. However, active implants are used at Wright-Patterson Air Force Base on specially trained pilots who have received millions of dollars in training. This bio-implant sends out an electronic signal if these pilots should have to parachute out of their planes.[4]

In 1994, Cuban and Haitian refugees were brought to Guantanamo, and the Deployable Mass Population Identification & Tracking System (DMPITS) was introduced. This DMPITS device consisted of a transponder wrist device that sent out an electronic signal so that the refugees could be tracked.

Many experts believe that it is the illegal immigration issue and the fear of child kidnapping that will cause the public to accept readily this kind of technology in the future. This new bio-implant technology and its related technologies are a multibillion-dollar business. There is no conspiracy to implement this technology. It is simply a fact that private corporations and government agencies are merging in a common effort to promote the technology. The gathering and selling of personal information in America has become a big business. Corporations routinely gather and sell databases on millions of individuals that contain information about the health, genetics, finances, employment history, political affiliations and religious beliefs of people.

In 1985, National Security Directive 145 allowed the National Security Agency (NSA) to have exclusive control over all federal computer databases. In addition, a National Identification Center has been established in Virginia. Over $392 million has been invested in this center, and the government expects that all states will be on-line by 1998. The highly secretive National Reconnaissance Center (NRO) in

Chantilly, Virginia, was recently constructed to house these and other operations.[5]

WORSHIP THE BEAST

Every person alive has a God-created capacity to worship God. If a person does not worship God, he or she will inevitably end up worshiping something else. Just look at what happens at a rock concert. Thousands of young people are not merely listening to music—they are worshiping the performers. Young people idolize these musicians and buy their CDs to listen to over and over again. Tragically, as they worship these pop stars they begin to follow them into immorality, drugs, rebellion and the New Age.

The Bible teaches us that before Satan fell he was God's worship leader in the spiritual realm. Satan knows all about the power in music to cause people to behave in certain ways. It is no accident that numerous music groups now have overtly satanic music and symbols that glorify the occult. Young people are being subtly prepared to worship the beast when he comes.

Eastern mysticism, the New Age and other counterfeit religious movements are preparing mankind for the eventual worship of the beast. In Revelation 13:8 it says, "All who dwell on the earth will worship him, whose names have not been written in the Book of Life of the Lamb slain from the foundation of the world." The Bible says that "all who dwell on the earth will worship him," and it is speaking of all those people alive during the Great

Tribulation who have rejected Jesus Christ as their Savior.

Can you imagine that billions of people alive during the Great Tribulation will deliberately reject God's message of salvation in Jesus Christ and choose to worship the Antichrist, Satan's direct representative? Make no mistake about it, beneath the thin veneer of "niceness" and social pleasantries of so-called ordinary middle-class people here in America and around the world exists a very deep and dark inner rebellion from God. You see, the Bible tells us that in fallen man "the heart of man is desperately wicked." Men and women who have not received the spirit of Jesus Christ into their lives are open to great spiritual deception.

This is why millions of people in our nation believe it is OK to abort babies, watch pornography and break the laws of God. Their hearts are in spiritual darkness. Even though they may wear designer clothes or drive a Lexus or a Mercedes, if they do not know Jesus Christ they are spiritually dead.

This deception and spiritual death will come to its fruition when an unbelieving mankind chooses to worship Satan instead of God.

WORSHIP AND THE ANTICHRIST

The earth will experience the most devastating judgment it has ever known in the Great Tribulation when the Antichrist steps into the rebuilt temple in Jerusalem and demands to be worshiped as God. This has been the satanic game plan since the beginning of time. Satan has always wanted to be God, and the Antichrist, whom Satan will possess, will demand that people worship him as God.

This is a pivotal point in human history. God is allowing the final fruition of mankind's rebellion, where a man who is Satan-possessed will claim to be God and cause the world to worship him. Essentially, humanism is the worship of man instead of God. This is a lot of what the self-esteem movement is all about. It is causing man to worship himself. This is what Satan promised Adam and Eve in the Garden of Eden—that they would be "like gods." The lie of humanism and the New Age Movement is that man is a god.

WORSHIPING ROBOT GODS

The Book of Revelation talks about people worshiping the image of the beast. Although many Bible scholars have speculated about what that means exactly, there are some who believe it refers to a kind of virtual reality or computer-generated image. Currently in India, the Hare Krishna Society has hired computer animators from the United States to build literal robots of Hindu gods that can move and talk. If you have ever been to Disneyland and have seen the robot of Abraham Lincoln speak, then you have an idea about how real these robots can look.

People will travel to this Hare Krishna temple to hear these robots created to look like Hindu gods speak to them. Could it be that this image of the beast in Revelation is making reference to some kind of virtual reality or computer-generated image?

ALIENS, DEMONS AND MACHINES

Many science-fiction writers and Hollywood film-makers are now writing about the merger of alien beings, demons and machines. The whole *Alien* film series with Sigourney Weaver captured imagery of the demon-like alien beings merging with high-tech machines. If you look at a lot of popular art work in our culture you will see an often repeated theme of aliens, demons and machine or computer-like technologies merging together. Art often forecasts our future.

The recent discoveries in artificial intelligence suggest that computers may eventually develop some kind of consciousness. It would not be far-fetched to suggest that demonic beings could take control of a computer's consciousness in the same way that a human being can be possessed by demons.

As we enter this End-Time scenario, we are seeing a blurring of the distinctions between the natural and supernatural. It is no accident that demonic entities, channeling, aliens, UFOs, spirit guides and the like are being manifested across our planet. The Book of Revelation tells us that one-third of the angels have revolted against God. It is these fallen beings that are responsible for all of these manifestations, and it is no accident that all of the messages these beings speak to mankind are perversions of the gospel of Jesus Christ. What we are seeing is a physical manifestation in our physical world of the fallen angels who are in rebellion from God. There may be an increasing merger between computer technologies and demons. The title of the rock album *Ghost in the Machine* suggests this. The increase of UFO sightings also could be some kind of blend between technology and demon activity.

The world will be seduced by the Antichrist because it has rejected Jesus Christ as God and has chosen to worship a man instead. This is a very heavy thing, and this great sin will unleash the fury of God's divine judgment upon this planet in what is called the Great Tribulation.

When the Antichrist betrays Israel and sets himself up in the rebuilt temple, he is declaring before the world that he is God. This is an act of ultimate rebellion by Satan, the powers of darkness and fallen mankind. This is where the power of sin will lead all of human history. Yet, it is precisely at this point that God will not allow this rebellion to continue any longer, and He will unleash powerful judgments upon the earth. However, the purpose of these judgments is to redeem and cause mankind to repent even until the very end.

SWEPT AWAY BY THE SUPERNATURAL

Jesus Christ warned that at the end of the age "false christs and false prophets will rise and show great signs and wonders to deceive, if possible even the elect" (Matt. 24:24). It seems that our society literally is being swept away by the supernatural. Hollywood movies dealing with supernatural themes and aliens from outer space are flooding the market place. Superstar John Travolta, who is a practicing Scientologist, claims that when he lays hands on people in a special technique they can be healed. Tom Cruise and Nicole Kidman of *Eyes Wide Shut* are also Scientologists.

Investigative reporter Bob Woodward discovered that Hillary Clinton has been consulting New Age psychic and teacher Jean Houston in order to contact Eleanor Roosevelt. In fact, it turns out that Hillary had been participating in a number of exercises designed to help her communicate with dead people. Her guide, Jean Houston, is not just some ordinary "pop psychologist." I remember her name from my "hippie" days. She advocated the use of psychedelic drugs and a number of other mystical activities.

Like many others of that generation, I experimented with LSD and other mind-altering drugs in order to "expand" my mind. However, it's one thing for a bunch of hippies to take the words of somebody like Houston seriously and an entirely different matter for someone like the First Lady to be experimenting with "altered states of consciousness" and consulting Eleanor Roosevelt in the writing of her book, *It Takes a Village*.

Hillary is not the only First Lady to experiment with the occult. Nancy Reagan regularly consulted astrologer Joanne Quigley. Both Hillary and Nancy have had profound influence on their husband's decisions. The fact that these powerful women are consulting mediums and astrologers says something about the nature of the battle in the invisible realm for our nation.

Oprah Winfrey, who is now one of the wealthiest women in America, has used her national talk show to promote many New Age teachers such as Marianne Williamson, who has been a spiritual advisor to First Lady Hillary Rodham Clinton. Oprah has embraced the occult teaching "A Course in Miracles" that is promoted by Marianne Williamson. "A Course in Miracles" presents a spiritual counterfeit of Christianity, although it uses terms like "miracles," "Son of God" and "Jesus Christ." Cher, Raquel Welch, Roseanne Arquette and countless other celebrities have attended her lectures. Williamson even officiated at the highly publicized wedding of Elizabeth Taylor at Michael Jackson's twenty-seven-hundred-acre fairy-tale estate in the Santa Ynez mountains.

Marianne Williamson's influence extends well beyond the Hollywood community. Her new book, *The Healing of America,* deals with politics and social change.[6] In the book she calls for a "new prophetic voice, not a soloist but a choir" and urges people to get involved with the ACLU and People for the American Way.

In an interview in *Magical Blend Magazine* Williamson states, "Both market-based and government-based political culture are basically coming from a mechanistic world view, which does not create genuine break-through."[7] Williamson understands that corporate America and our government do not really have any real answers for the people and that only a spiritual revolution will save us from self-destruction. The only problem is that Williamson's answers come out of an occult world view—not a Christian one.

There are powerful spirits of deception at work in our

nation that are eager to lead us astray and bring us into captivity. Eventually, this rise in the supernatural is leading us to the time talked about in Revelation 13:11–14, where it says:

> Then I saw another beast coming up out of the earth, and he had two horns like a lamb and spoke like a dragon. And he exercises all the authority of the first beast in his presence, and causes the earth and those who dwell in it to worship the first beast, whose deadly wound was healed. He performs great signs, so that he even makes fire come down from heaven on the earth in the sight of men. And he deceives those who dwell on the earth by those signs which he was granted to do in the sight of the beast, telling those who dwell on the earth to make an image to the beast who was wounded by the sword and lived.

This passage of scripture is speaking about the false prophet, who is the Antichrist's spokesperson. This false prophet will have the power to perform supernatural signs in order to deceive people and cause them to worship the Antichrist. The occult, false religions, counterfeit supernatural power and the entire movement of mystical religions is moving toward the time when they will play key roles in the false prophet's plan of spiritual deception.

The Bible teaches us very clearly that there is a war going on in the spiritual or invisible realm between God and Satan. In this warfare, there are renegade spiritual beings who are attempting to deceive mankind from the truth of the gospel of Jesus Christ.

*It was granted to him to make war
with the saints and to overcome them.
And authority was given him over every
tribe, tongue, and nation.*

—Revelation 13:7

NATO, Kosovo and Global Government

I N REVELATION 13:7 we read how the Antichrist will have authority over the entire world. Daniel 7:23 says that the Antichrist "shall devour the whole earth." Many people have speculated as to what role organizations like the United Nations may play in a global government set up by the Antichrist. Others strongly believe that the Antichrist and the revived Roman Empire will come out of a United European Community. In any case, the Antichrist will end up controlling the whole world.

If the Antichrist emerges out of a United Europe, as the Bible seems to indicate, his global government will encompass the whole world. The initial systems of this global government are already being put in place. A world economy, the coming cashless society, the Internet and the push toward globalism by major multinational corporations are all setting up the climate for some kind of global government.

Ironically, it is not just what the dominant media call "antigovernment extremists" who fear totalitarianism and global government here in our nation and around the world. Movie director Oliver Stone has constantly exposed totalitarian trends in his films. The late William Burroughs, who wrote the novel *Naked Lunch* and who along with Allen Ginsberg and Jack Kerouac founded what was called the "Beat Generation," said, "I think the United States is heading in the direction of a socialist police state similar to England and not too different than Russia."[1]

It is amazing to see the number of leftist-leaning writers, authors and thinkers who see the handwriting on the wall in terms of global government and the loss of our freedoms. Anybody who studies history and current events can see where our world is headed, and that is precisely what the Bible predicted thousands of years ago. It is no accident that historical, economic, political and social trends are now setting the stage for some kind of global Antichrist government.

The war in Kosovo is another step in that direction. Globalist groups like the Bilderbergers are using that war to establish global control incrementally. The European Union, NATO, the United Nations and other groups are cooperating in this effort. Many in Israel fear that a global army will move into Israel to establish "peace" just like it did in Kosovo.

NATO AND KOSOVO

Although many people seem to think that the United Nations will establish a world government, there are many biblical prophecies that seem to indicate that the coming world government will form out of Europe. The recent war in Kosovo gave rise to the renewed role by NATO in becoming the world's police force.

The North Atlantic Treaty Organization was formed in 1949 and had its fiftieth anniversary in 1999. The war against Kosovo is just the beginning of a whole range of expanded powers that NATO has assumed for itself. NATO has become the police force for the United Europe, with military powers not only in Europe, but in North Africa, Algeria, Tunisia, Libya, Egypt, Lebanon, Syria, Egypt, Jordan and Israel. NATO represents a single European voice in military matters. What happened in Kosovo was that a nation attempted to be sovereign outside of the European Union or NATO. As a result of openly defying this United Europe, it was crushed militarily. The legality of this came out of the Amsterdam Treaty, signed in June of 1977, which strengthened the role of a European Union in military matters.

One of the chief negotiators in Kosovo, Strobe Talbott, who works for the Clinton Administration, is an ardent globalist. Like many in our nation's government, Talbott does not owe his allegiance to the United States but to a new international order. As a deputy secretary in the United States State Department, he openly proclaims that his interest is not the United States but internationalism. Talbott states, "All countries are basically social arrangements, accommodations to changing circumstances... They are all artificial and temporal." Talbott suggests that the European Union is a "pioneer" of "supranational" regional cohesion that could pave the way for globalism.[2]

KOSOVO TO GOG AND MAGOG

A number of analysts of current affairs believe that the United States and NATO's war in Kosovo is a dress rehearsal for what could happen against Israel in the near future. Over a year ago, the Bilderberger group met to plan a war in Kosovo. Now the Bilderbergers are meeting in Portugal to plan global governance, the formation of an Asian bloc led by Japan, the replacement of NATO with a Western European army and events in the Middle East.

Many analysts and Jews living in Israel believe that U.S., NATO, United Nations and globalist forces are poised to invade the Middle East and Israel in the same way they invaded Kosovo. It is not inconceivable to think of European, U.S. and United Nations forces landing in Israel to enforce some kind of peace settlement, the declaration of a Palestinian state and the final disposition of Jerusalem. For years globalists have been working behind the scenes, pressuring Israel to give up land for peace in Israel and to allow for the creation of a Palestinian state in Israel, with its capital in Jerusalem.

With Kosovo as a dry run, it is not difficult to imagine U.S., U.N. and NATO forces moving into Israel to keep the peace. It also would not be difficult to see Russia moving into Israel with Muslim allies and U.S., U.N. and NATO forces intervening.

Ezekiel 38 talks about an End-Time battle called the war of Gog and Magog. Some believe this is part of the battle of Armageddon; others believe it will be a separate battle. But given the state of current events, it is not difficult to conceive a scenario where Israel is invaded, and God supernaturally destroys Israel's enemies, as prophesied in Ezekiel 38. It is prophesied that at that time not only Israel will know that God defended it, but the whole world will be faced with that reality. Ezekiel 38:23 states, "Thus I will magnify Myself and sanctify Myself, and I will be known in the eyes of many nations. Then they shall know that I am the LORD."

This will cause a spiritual rebirth in Israel. "'And I will not hide My face from them anymore; for I shall have poured out My Spirit on the house of Israel,' says the Lord GOD" (Ezek. 39:29).

THE GROWLING BEAR

The prophet Ezekiel also predicted that in the last days a nation to the uttermost north of Israel, which is Russia, would invade Israel. Russia is in serious trouble. With Boris Yeltsin's health rapidly failing, men like Yevgeny M. Primakov are waiting for the chance to take over. Primakov was the man responsible for the billion-dollar loan from the Arab states in the Persian Gulf.

The International Monetary Fund recently loaned Russia over $10 billion in order to keep its economy afloat. But reports keep emerging out of Russia that IMF loans went straight into an offshore company called the Financial Management Company Ltd. (FIMACO). A former KGB officer, Colonel Leonid Veselovsky, stated that the money was funneled into offshore havens to insure that Communist Party leaders were taken care of after they lost power.[3]

In addition, Russia owed around $9.1 billion in arms, fighter planes and submarine costs to nations like China. But the Russian economy is still faltering. Compounding the problem is that Russia has been having very poor grain harvests. A giant military move in the Middle East to form an alliance with nations like Iran would gain them control of the world's oil. Part of the deal might be the takeover of Israel in order to satisfy the militant Islamic nations who would be part of this alliance.

Is Russia Preparing to Attack the United States?

Bill Lee, a former official with the Defense Intelligence Agency, has estimated that Russia has between ten thousand and twelve thousand antiballistic missiles in its defense system. In addition, Russia has been conducting a series of nuclear war exercises called "West 99" and "Combat Commonwealth 99." These defense drills are designed to prepare Russia for any U.S. missile and bomb strikes against their nation. In addition, Russia has been building a vast system of underground bunkers and nuclear blast shelters. Some intelligence experts are speculating that Russia is secretly preparing for World War III.[4]

Some military experts believe that Russia may be making preparations for an attack on the United States. The Russians have been storing grain, foodstuffs, gold, oil and diesel fuel. Russian underground bunkers can store 326 million tons of grain, and their military can store another 80 million tons of grain.[5]

Simultaneously with the Russian buildup, the Clinton Administration has been disarming the United States and pushing for the "Comprehensive Test Ban Treaty." President Clinton believes this is urgent for our national security. Critics of the nuclear test ban bill believe it would tie our hands.

Russia continues to prepare for the possibility of a nuclear war with the United States. Since the 1960s the Russians have been building underground bunkers in case of a nuclear war. In addition, Russia has a giant underground complex the size of Washington, D.C., called "Evil Mountain," or Yamantau Mountain. The purpose of "Evil Mountain" is to enable the Russian elite to survive a nuclear war. The Clinton Administration has concealed these developments from the American people in order to promote START I, II and III treaties.[6]

The new military buildup in Russia, along with the increased problems between Israel and some of her neighbors, seems to indicate an eventual fulfillment of an

Ezekiel 38 scenario. Russia is committed to backing militant Islamic nations in the Middle East. At some point the Bible states the Russian bear will move south to invade Israel with a confederation of militant Islamic nations.[7]

Perhaps our government is attempting to send signals to nations like Russia, China and North Korea that we are prepared for nuclear war. Driving to church on a Saturday night with my wife and children, we looked up into the sky and saw a missile shooting into the air. Minutes later a second missile hit the first missile, completely lighting up the night sky. I had never seen anything like this in my life. The next morning the *Los Angeles Times* reported that the Department of Defense fired an unarmed ballistic missile from the Marshall Islands. A second missile, a Minuteman II, was launched from Vandenberg Air Force Base and destroyed the first missile.

For all the nations have
drunk the maddening wine of
her adulteries.

—REVELATION 18:3, NIV

One World—an Idea Whose Time Has Come?

I N RESPONSE TO the criticism that has come against the Clinton White House over foreign-linked contributions, Alvin and Heidi Toffler, the authors of *The Third Wave, Powershift* and *Future Shock,* have defended the White House on the basis of a globalist philosophy, which they embrace.[1]

The Tofflers said in a *Los Angeles Times* commentary:

> Indeed, the concept that foreign-linked funding is necessarily inappropriate is based on the obsolete conceptions of both sovereignty and nationhood. It is based on the idea that states have absolute sovereignty and that nations are closed systems. All

of that is coming apart as we move into a global economy.[2]

The Tofflers go on to suggest that "transnational flows of political influence will increase." They close the article by declaring, "For good or ill, it is time we recognize that politics, too, like economics and information is going transnational." According to the Tofflers' reasoning, it's OK for a nation like Communist China to buy influence because we live in a new global economy. What this really means is that our democratic form of government can be subverted by any foreign agent if they are willing to spend the money. What used to be considered treasonous is now acceptable, because after all the reasoning goes, "Everything is going transnational."

Make no mistake about it, this means the end of democracy as we know it and the demise of America as an independent and free nation state. For centuries America has been unique among the nations because she has been a democracy built on Judeo-Christian values. Now America is being merged into a new form of "global governance," which is no longer democratic and built on Judeo-Christian values. Instead of democracy, we will be ruled by an elite group, and instead of Judeo-Christian values we will have humanism. Welcome to the new world order!

GLOBAL CONSCIOUSNESS

Many of us grew up in a time when strong patriotic

feelings about America were not only common but encouraged by the media and our educational systems. The heroes of yesterday's movies, like John Wayne, were fiercely patriotic and unashamed of the American flag. Things have changed dramatically in the last few decades. It is no longer "in" to be patriotic or "proud to be an American" as it once was.

Former presidents Jimmy Carter and Gerald Ford, along with 137 senior government and business officials, signed full-page ads in the *New York Times* and the *Washington Post* calling for the United States to do such things as refinance the International Monetary Fund, pay back United Nation's dues and give the president fast-track authority to negotiate trade agreements and preserve the treasury's right to make international loans. The ad read, "A Time for American Leadership on Key Global Issues."[3]

Although it is obvious that we now live in a global economy and that America needs to compete in a global marketplace, there are some dangerous trends in this push to globalism. First of all, there will be a reduction of U.S. national sovereignty and, along with it, a loss of personal and religious freedoms that our Constitution and Bill of Rights guarantee. Second, in this new globalist society there is no Constitution or Bill of Rights. The danger is that Internationalists are attempting to subvert these rights through a series of secret U.N. treaties, which in some cases do away with our rights as Americans.

Millions in our nation have been brainwashed by the

mass media and the educational system to think of themselves as citizens of the world or the planet. John Reed, who is the chairman and CEO of Citicorp, gave a speech at Georgetown University that was televised by CSPAN.[4] Reed referred to himself as a "global citizen" and explained that when he was making major economic decisions, he thought of the welfare of workers in foreign nations just as much as he did about U.S. workers.

It was disturbing in Reed's talk that apparently he did not believe in America, but rather the world. Here is a man in charge of billions of dollars and the head of a major multinational corporation who views himself not as a U.S. citizen but as a "global citizen." The tragedy is that Reed's thinking is reflective of a major paradigm shift in consciousness of those who run our nation and control our most powerful institutions.

John Reed constantly used terms like "commonality" and spoke of the 950 million people on Planet Earth who were part of economically developing nations such as the United States, Japan and Europe as well as of the 3 billion people who were in more primitive nations. Reed's perspective was global, and he was in favor of instituting common accounting standards so that trillions of dollars could flow from the various markets unhindered.

When Reed spoke he revealed a very profound change in the way many people now think about themselves and the world. He did not see himself as an American but as a planetary citizen. This shift in consciousness is increasingly common among the elite in education, industry, government and the arts. In fact, it is this change of consciousness that will usher in a new world order and some kind of global government in the near future. Many people make the mistake of thinking that global government will be the result of some dark conspiracy. In reality, global government will arise because of new belief systems and philosophies.

In actuality, those who control major multinational corporations, education, the media and government already see themselves as global citizens. They view such things as patriotism and nationalism as regressive ideas from the past. There is a plan underway to phase our nation and other nations in the world into this new global government gradually. This elite group understands that patriotic feelings and nationalistic sentiments are still very strong in America and other places around the world. For that reason, the goal of a new world order and global government will be phased into position. We are now in the initial phases of seeing that plan implemented. The recent meeting in Sinatra, Portugal, by the Bilderberger group, which featured key United States Senators, the heads of media and the movers and shakers of business, points to a coming global government.

*The fourth beast shall be a fourth kingdom
on earth, which shall be different from
all other kingdoms, and shall devour
the whole earth.*

—Daniel 7:23

15

Europe United

I N THE BOOK of Daniel and the Book of Revelation are specific references to a revived Roman Empire in the last days that would occupy roughly the same geographic areas that the ancient Roman Empire occupied. I believe that new European Union is the revival of this ancient Roman Empire and the "fourth beast" that both Daniel and Revelation talk about. The Bible also makes reference to a single currency in the last days. The creation of a single currency, the "euro" is an important step in this development. One *USA Today* article expressed the sentiment of many global economists when he stated, "For the first time since the Roman

Empire, we will soon share the same money—the euro."[1]

Currently there are fifteen nations in the European Union, and they are moving toward the goal of creating a single European currency, or "euro-dollar." United Europe's bank is launching a competition to design a new single currency called the *euro,* which will be available beginning in January 2002. The European Monetary Institute (EMI) has assembled a group of experts that include pyschologists to agree on a new bank note that will be acceptable by all fifteen-member countries. It will be a difficult task, because all of the member nations would like to see some kind of symbol representing their nation on the new euro notes.

Back in December of 1991, in the Dutch town of Maastricht, the Maastricht Treaty was signed, creating an economic and monetary union called the European Union (EU). One of the key components of this union is the final implementation of a single currency. Originally, the Maastricht Treaty called for a single currency by 1997. Now the target date is hopefully set for 2002.

Although there has been a great deal of "euro-euphoria" manufactured largely by the European press, there has been a grassroots backlash. As evidence of that backlash, Dutch Finance Minister Gerrit Zalm, a promoter of the European Monetary Union (EMU) received a pie in the face, which was televised by the BBC. Yet the powerful forces who back the EMU are not about to be dissuaded with public opinion. With fifteen members in the EU, eleven have joined the EMU, including Austria, Belgium, Finland, France, Germany, Ireland, Italy, Luxembourg, the Netherlands, Portugal and Spain.

Going back to the 1920s when Britain was controlled by an elite group of financiers, even then plans were being made for a United Europe. Investment bankers who were part of the Rhodes-Milner Group took control of the media, education, business and political parties. It was the dream of Cecil Rhodes, a British millionaire, to see the establishment of a socialist-style world government. Later the Rothschilds, J. P. Morgan and the Rockefeller empires helped finance the institutions that laid the groundwork for a United Europe. Behind the scenes, many of the same financial interests that established the Royal Institute for International Affairs and the Council on Foreign Relations have controlling financial interests here in the United States, Europe and Asia.

After World War II, these international bankers promoted the Marshall Plan in Europe, which was financed by American taxpayers under the guise of stopping Communism. The Treaty of Rome was created along with the Common Market.

One of the stumbling blocks to the acceptance of the euro note has been the loss of sovereignty. Monetary policy would be set by a supranational European central bank. In addition, once the authority of the European Monetary Institute (EMI) is in place, a United States of Europe will have arisen, for all practical purposes.

A United States of Europe will become the most

powerful economic force in the world today. The United States of America has been attempting to use its influence to restrict the goals of the Maastricht Treaty. The United States has zealously been pushing for the goal of global free trade. A single European currency would quickly become a second international reserve currency side by side with a weakening U.S. dollar. The European Union has a population of 373 million vs. the United States, which only has a population of 265 million. In addition, the total GDP of the European Union is $8.6 trillion vs. that of the United States, which is $7.3 trillion.

DANGEROUS TRENDS IN EUROPE

In Cologne, Germany, there has been intense government persecution of Christian churches. If this activity goes unchecked, a tremendous wave of anti-Christian sentiment could follow, spreading throughout Europe. Prophetically, if a "revived Roman Empire" is to emerge out of a United Europe, with the Antichrist coming to power over this new Europe, it would fit into the prophetic puzzle that Europe would be increasingly anti-Christian and anti-Semitic.

In Vitrolles, France, the National Front, a political party with fascist leanings, has taken over the local government. The Front has taken over three cities in areas of France. The goal of the Front is "France for the French," and it wants to get rid of three million immigrants.[2] All across Europe there is a resurgence of anti-Semitic, fascist and neo-Nazi political groups. An anti-Semitic sentiment is brewing once again across the land, and certain government agencies are attacking Christian groups as well.

We have seen that Europe, Russia and Israel will play vital roles in End-Time events—as well as the United States. What about China?

Then the sixth angel sounded: And I heard a voice from the four horns of the golden altar which is before God, saying to the sixth angel who had the trumpet, "Release the four angels who are bound at the great river Euphrates." So the four angels, who had been prepared for the hour and day and month and year, were released to kill a third of mankind. Now the number of the army of the horsemen was two hundred million; I heard the number of them.

—REVELATION 9:13–16

China's Kings From the East

MANY BIBLE SCHOLARS believe this army of two hundred million men mentioned in the Book of Revelation will come from China. In Revelation 16:12 the Bible talks about "the kings from the east." In Greek, *east* is translated as "kings of the rising sun," which is a clear reference to China. It is no accident that China now has the largest standing army in the world and that its economy is steadily growing. While nations like the United States continue to falter economically, nations like China are enjoying unprecedented growth due to its cheap labor pool.

China has become the third largest economy in the world after the United States and Japan.

CHINESE SPIES IN AMERICA

China has been actively spying on the United States and stealing information from our secret weapons labs. The CIA has reported that China may have stolen nuclear secrets from Los Alamos and from other weapons labs across the country. When the CIA showed the information to a team of top nuclear weapons experts, these experts went into a state of shock—the Chinese had stolen our most sensitive weapons secrets![1]

It seems the Chinese have managed to get up-to-date information on seven U.S. nuclear warheads, and in an attempt to copy the technology, they have acquired two cruise missiles that were shot at Osama bin Laden but failed to detonate. All intelligence reports seem to indicate that China is mobilizing an all-out effort to build up its military machine and defense technology. It doesn't take a rocket scientist to figure out that we are on their "hit list," and that as a Communist nation they have global ambitions.

WHY WE CONTINUE TO PLAY BALL WITH CHINA

China has been given the "most-favored nation" status by the United States government. Although the advantages of trading with China have been considerably played up by advocates of GATT and the media, the reality is that the United States purchases about $40 billion a year from China, and they buy about $10 billion a year from us, which leaves us with a trade deficit of nearly $30 billion a year.

William Greider, author of *One World, Ready or Not: The*

Manic Logic of Global Capitalism, warns that China's slave labor gives them the ability to underbid everyone in the global marketplace.[2] The amount of goods coming into the United States from China is staggering. Much of that money is used to build up their military machine.

What the dominant media has not told you is that a number of leading American Fortune 500 companies that have significant business interests in China have hired a public relations firm to make relations with China look very attractive. These Fortune 500 companies have turned a blind eye to the ruthless persecution of Christians in China and have spent over $100 million selling Americans on the idea that it is in our best interest to partner with China. In addition, these American multinational corporations have lined many or our politicians' pockets in both the Democratic and Republican parties in order to protect their deals with China.

The Democratic National Committee has reportedly received millions of dollars in Chinese money from a variety of front organizations. Not only did President Clinton's legal defense fund receive money, but the DNC spent over $42 million in television commercials in order to get Clinton and Gore reelected. It seems that the White House and our politicians are up for sale, even if it jeopardizes the national security of our nation.

Americans have constantly been told that the Chinese will purchase things like American cars and that it will be good for us if we become active trading partners. However, the average Chinese worker makes about thirty cents per hour, and it takes them about two years to save up for a bicycle. Obviously, people who make these kind of wages can hardly afford to buy cars from us. Also, a large percentage of Chinese products are made in the over 3,100 slave labor camps where the workers are not paid at all. Many Bible-believing Christians have been sent to these camps for their religious beliefs and are forced to work long hours while being imprisoned.

Not only has our government turned a blind eye toward these prison camps and the enslavement of Christian believers, but it is impossible for American workers to compete against an economy built on slave labor and workers earning only thirty cents an hour. This economic advantage has caused billions of dollars to pour into the Chinese economy.

China will continue to play an increasingly important role in the next few decades. The military exercises that China conducted against Taiwan signaled to the world that China is a powerful and potential nuclear threat. For a nation that cannot properly clothe or feed her people, China spends over $28 billion a year on its military. China maintains nearly 3 million troops with over 1.2 million reservists. The population of China is 1.2 billion people, of which a growing number is male due to the government-sponsored abortion program based on sex selection. The government encourages Chinese families to give birth to males while aborting female babies. By the year 2000 A.D., if this trend continues there will be tens of millions of men who will not be to able to have wives or families.

Part of the reason that China is able to maintain the largest standing army in the world is due to its enormous population and its surplus of draftable males. But China produces this excess of males through forced abortions and sterilization of its people. Just two hours north of Los Angeles, in a place called Lerdo Prison, eight women who fled China's forced abortion and sterilization are locked up by order of the United States government.

In 1990 President George Bush issued an executive order allowing political asylum for refugees fleeing China's population-control program. In January of 1993 President Bill Clinton, a strong supporter of the Abortion Rights movement, reversed the Bush order. In June of 1993 a boat filled with refugees from China, called the *Golden Venture,* docked in New York with 286 illegal Chinese immigrants. Many of these people were fleeing China's oppressive abortion and sterilization programs. The eight Chinese women locked up in Lerdo Prison were on this boat.[3]

Although the U.S. government allows tens of thousands of illegal aliens to come across the border of Mexico, and the media has expressed its politically correct outrage over the fact that policemen beat the illegal aliens in a pickup truck after a high-speed car chase, the eight Chinese women in Lerdo Prison have been ignored by the government and the media because they are politically in-correct. They dared to risk their lives by not submitting to the pro-abortion policies of the Chinese government.

In September of 1995, when Hillary Clinton addressed the U.N.'s Fourth World Conference on Women in Beijing,

China, she publicly denounced sex-selected abortion, forced abortion and sterilization. But privately, the Clinton Administration continues to leave the Chinese women locked up in Lerdo Prison. Even after a fifty-day hunger strike, they remain behind bars for committing the crime of fleeing a totalitarian government that wants to brutally sterilize them and force them to have abortions.[4]

Despite China's treatment of Taiwan, its numerous human rights' abuses ranging from forcing Christians and others to work in slave labor camps making toys and other products for the Western world and its program of forced abortions and sterilization, our government recently voted to give China a "favored-nation status." In a new world order based on political expediency and economic profit over human values, China, despite the fact that it is still an evil Communist dictatorship, is treated with respect and is welcomed as a trading partner.

China's cheap labor, which often comes from prison camps, is giving the nation an outstanding economic growth of 13 percent annually. Just walk into any toy store or clothing store and read the labels to see how many of these products are made in China.

Some Bible scholars believe that nations such as China, Russia, Israel, the United States and others comprise a world system called biblical Babylon. Others see Babylon differently. Let's take a look.

After these things I saw another angle coming down from heaven ... saying, "Babylon the great is fallen, is fallen, and has become a dwelling place of demons, a prison for every foul spirit, and a cage for every unclean and hated bird! For all the nations have drunk of the wine of the wrath of her fornication, the kings of the earth have committed fornication with her, and the merchants of the earth have become rich through the abundance of her luxury."

—Revelation 18:1–3

The Fall
of Babylon

F OR MANY YEARS Bible scholars have been debating whether Babylon will actually be the rebuilt city of ancient Babylon or whether it represents a symbol of the political, spiritual and economic might of this present world system, which encompasses all the nations about which we have spoken.

Nevertheless, isn't it interesting that Saddam Hussein has largely rebuilt the city of ancient Babylon in modern-day Iraq? Hussein has invested close to $1 billion in a massive rebuilding program of palaces, hotels and walls.

Although publicly Saddam Hussein claims to be a good Muslin, many sources report that he is involved in the occult and witchcraft. He sees Iraq as a modern-day Babylon, the city that was one of the world's greatest political, economic and military powers of its day. Nimrod, whose name means "revolt," built the Tower of Babel in order to start a one-world religion. He established the city of Babylon in order to create a one-world government. God destroyed the Tower of Babel and confused their common language.

Whether or not this actual city of Babylon will become the Babylon in the Book of Revelation remains to be seen. But the push toward a global centralized government and a one-world religion that will be ruled by the Antichrist is a return to ancient Babylonianism under Nimrod. The Bible predicts that this Babylonian system will be destroyed by God suddenly. (See Jeremiah 51:8; Revelation 18:1–9.) According to Isaiah 13:19–22, Babylon was to be completely destroyed and uninhabited. This theme is repeated in Jeremiah 51:24–26, 61–64. Some Bible scholars have pointed out that ancient Babylon as a city was not destroyed until centuries after the empire disintegrated. As such, none of these prophecies have been fulfilled.

Isaiah 13:19–22 indicates that the fall of Babylon would occur in the day of the Lord, which lends credence to the belief that a rebuilt Babylon will play a significant role in the last days. Could Saddam Hussein's plans and defeat play a significant role in Bible prophecy?

THE RETURN OF SADDAM HUSSEIN

The one thing about Saddam Hussein is that he is not

stupid. Although the Clinton Administration and the world press touted the success of the Russians in "brokering" a peace deal with Iraq, the reality is that this "Desert Fox" simply bought time to move his biological and chemical weapons out of the way to where U.N. inspection forces could not find them. Secretary of State Madeleine Albright and other government officials later agreed to lift some of the sanctions against Iraq in order to secure peace.

During the Gulf War, the United States and other allied nations made the mistake of not completely destroying Saddam Hussein's military operation. As a result, the Clinton Administration has had to take on this madman again. Iraq currently has approximately 400,000 troops, 250 Russian combat aircraft, Scud missiles and mobile launchers in the Persian Gulf Region. The United States has only 20,000 troops (many of whom are on ships), 270 warplanes, 50 helicopters, Cruise missiles, B-52 bombers and a number of aircraft carriers in the region.

Although the Iraqi newspaper *Babel* (the same name as the Tower of Babel in the Bible) states, "We shall defend our sovereignty with our nails and teeth," the Clinton Administration has launched back-to-back cruise missile attacks on Iraq.[1]

THE WORLD TRADE CENTER, SADDAM'S REVENGE?

Saddam Hussein is not the complete lunatic that the American media portrays him to be. He is crafty and cunning and has developed ways of getting back at the United States, despite the Bush and Clinton Administrations' public claims of victory. Salah al-Mukhtar, editor of Iraq's *Al Jumhuriya* newspaper, said, "Let the United States hear well…Don't imagine that by destroying our missiles you stripped us of our ability to act, because every Iraqi is a missile that can reach countries and cities…If you want, we will become everything that is frightening to you."[2]

According to inside reports, the majority of law enforcement officers in New York City believe that Saddam Hussein and Iraq were directly involved in the World Trade Center bombing. There is increasing evidence to suggest that Iraq had infiltrated Sheik Omar's group and helped them to build the bomb. Sheik Omar and his followers then became the fall guys for the WTC bombing.

SLEEPERS

Intelligence reports suggest that Iraq has placed what are called "sleepers" in key cities around the United States. A *sleeper* is a hidden intelligence or terrorist operative who remains hidden until he or she is needed to participate in a clandestine operation. Some intelligence experts believe that there was an Iraqi sleeper involved in the WTC bombing. Many believe that this Iraqi sleeper is a scientist working in the field of genetic engineering somewhere in New York City. This scientist may have access to high-security laboratories. Suppose this Iraqi sleeper became involved in a biological warfare operation.[3]

A BIOLOGICAL WARFARE COVER-UP?

Many American servicemen who were involved in

Operation Desert Storm have become sick with strange illnesses. Some of these military personnel have reportedly infected their families and people in their communities. There is a growing number of doctors and military personnel who believe that thousands of our servicemen who were involved in Operation Desert Storm were infected with deadly biological warfare agents by Saddam Hussein. In addition, some doctors and servicemen have suggested that there has been a giant government cover-up over this whole issue.

On June 21, 1996, in a major reversal the Pentagon admitted that it has evidence that an Iraqi bunker at Kamisiyah just north of Kuwait contained nerve and mustard gas. When this was blown up by U.S. soldiers, the gas could have drifted down on American soldiers, causing an assortment of symptoms known as Gulf War Syndrome. Strangely, the Pentagon has contradicted itself a number of times regarding biological warfare in the Persian Gulf.[4]

There were a number of incidents in military actions where poison gas alarms went off. But the official story was that these were false alarms. So far, out of the 697,000 Gulf veterans, 10,142 have claimed sickness from the Gulf War. A 1974 treatise titled "Delayed Toxic Effects of Chemical Warfare Agents," by Dr. Karlheinz Lohs, former director of the Institute of Chemical Toxicology of the East German Academy of Sciences, listed symptoms such as neurological, gastrointestinal, heart problems, loss of memory and a greater risk of cancer—the same symptoms found in soldiers suffering from the Gulf War Syndrome.[5]

THE BRUTAL REALITY

If Iran, Iraq, Syria or any other nation decided to attack Israel in some kind of collective military action, the brutal reality is that the United States government, the United Nations or the European Community would probably do very little to interfere with any military action. The reason for this is that our military intelligence understands that agents for these governments have the capacity to come into the United States with suitcases of chemical, biological or nuclear weapons and destroy our civilian population through a terrorist attack. In addition, the intelligence community knows that more than forty-three "suitcase nuclear weapons" are missing from the Soviet arsenal and are most likely in the hands of nations like Iran and other countries that promote terrorism.

The attack in Luxor, Egypt, where terrorists killed sixty tourists at the Temple of Hatsheput, is only the tip of the iceberg. Muslim extremists are attempting to force the Egyptian government to bow to its demands, and they understand that tourism is one of the main industries of a nation like Egypt.

As we have seen, the nations of the world are lining up politically, socially and morally according to the Book of Revelation. You may be wondering, *If the Armageddon clock countdown is ticking nearer and nearer to global midnight, what should we who are living on earth expect? What is coming? Can we prepare? Are we ready?* Let's examine these questions.

Section III
Are We Ready
for What Is Coming?

For then there will be a great tribulation,
such as has not occurred since the
beginning of the world until now,
nor ever shall.

—MATTHEW 24:21, NAS

18

Such As Has Not Occurred Until Now— the Great Tribulation

N OBODY KNOWS FOR sure exactly where we are on the prophetic timeline. We may enter a holding pattern, and this whole thing may be delayed. We must remember that Christians in times past were convinced that people like Napoleon and Adolph Hitler were the Antichrist. So no matter how convinced we are of our analysis of Bible prophecy, we have to approach the whole thing with humility and a recognition that in our humanness we can be prone to error. I do not want anyone to read the pages of this book and go out and buy a camouflage outfit, bottled water or a jeep and begin heading for the hills.

But at some point in history, the world is going to enter

into what the Bible calls the Tribulation period. Those who hold to a premillennial, pretribulational Rapture point of view believe that believers in Jesus Christ will be raptured before the Tribulation. In fact, according to the premillennial, pretribulational Rapture perspective, the Tribulation begins when the church of Jesus Christ is raptured from Planet Earth. When this happens, a seven-year Tribulation period begins where the Antichrist will assume control. Three and one-half years into the Tribulation the Antichrist will betray Israel and demand that he be worshiped as God in a rebuilt Jewish temple.

I know many strong and sincere believers who hold different positions as to the timing of the Rapture. Some believe in a premillennial, midtribulation Rapture or a premillennial post-tribulational Rapture.

Personally, I believe that God is going to remove His people before the Tribulation. In the same way that God removed Noah from destruction in the ark during the flood, I believe that Jesus Christ is our ark, and that before the Tribulation begins He will remove us from the earth.

However, this does not mean that I believe that the church of Jesus Christ will be immune from difficulty, persecution and even death as we grow closer to that date. Some people, especially in America, have twisted the message of a pretribulation Rapture to mean that the minute things get tough here in America and around the world, God is going to remove us in the Rapture. I discussed this with Pat Robertson, founder of the Christian Broadcasting Network, when he was a guest on my radio program.

Robertson believes that many Christians in America are in for a rude awakening.[1]

There is a growing anti-Christian sentiment here in America and around the world. As men's hearts grow darker there will be an increased hatred for Christians in this world. Here in our own nation we see the emergence of powerful anti-Christian forces in government, political movements and social causes. There are growing numbers of people in our society who hate the Bible, Jesus Christ and Christians. Given the right circumstances, economic conditions and political climate, the level of animosity against believers could be greatly accelerated. In our own nation we could see beatings, imprisonment, death and widescale persecution of believers. The murders of Christians worshiping God in a church in Texas and the anti-Christian art at the Brooklyn Museum in New York reflect a growing hostility against Christianity.

The Bible does not teach that Christians in America will be immune to such difficulties if these things should happen. Although it is a positive thing to look forward to the "blessed hope" and to be able to trust God for deliverance, the teaching of a pretribulation Rapture should never be misconstrued to teach escapism and irresponsibility. Jesus Christ taught us to "occupy until [He] come[s]" (Luke 19:13, KJV) It is vital that Christians pray, fast, intercede and actively stand up for what it right in our nation.

I do not believe it is God's will for Christians to give this nation over into the hands of darkness.

For they are spirits of demons, performing signs, which go out to the kings of the earth and of the whole world, to gather them to the battle of that great day of God Almighty. "Behold, I am coming as a thief. Blessed is he who watches, and keeps his garments, lest he walk naked and they see his shame." And they gathered them together to the place called in Hebrew, Armageddon.

—Revelation 16:14–16

19

On the Road to Armageddon

W HEN THE SIXTH bowl of wrath is poured out, spirits of demons performing signs are going to be sent out to the "kings of the earth and of the whole world" to gather them to the battle of Armageddon. *Armageddon,* or "Harmageddon," may refer to the Mount of Megiddo, at the entrance of the Plain of Esdraelon in the northern parts of Jezreel, the site of one of Israel's key battlefields in history.

In actuality, Armageddon will not just be one battle, but it will be a series of battles. It will unfold as demons who are under the control of Satan, the Antichrist and the false prophet seduce the world's rulers through powerful miracles to fight against Israel and Jesus Christ. Some Bible scholars believe that the War of Gog and Magog in Ezekiel 38 is part of this battle. Others believe that the War of Gog and Magog will occur before Armageddon.

WORLD WAR III

At the beginning of the Great Tribulation, a world government will be created under the rulership of the Antichrist. This world government will consist of a revived Roman Empire of ten nations that will rule the entire globe. It seems that about seven years after this world government is put in place, there will be some kind of power struggle between the Antichrist and other nations. The nations of the world will be led by powerful demonic forces to converge at Armageddon. It appears they will be challenging the world government of the Antichrist and contending for power. It may well be that the hidden agenda of the demonic spirits is to marshal a global military force to battle against Jesus Christ and the armies of heaven.

In Revelation 19:11–21, we read the account of how Jesus Christ will come from heaven on a white horse along with the armies of heaven to defeat the beast and the kings of the earth.

The beast and the false prophet will be captured and cast into the lake of fire (Rev. 19:20). In Revelation 19:19 it states, "And I saw the beast, the kings of the earth, and their armies, gathered together to make war against Him who sat on the horse and against His army." Can you imagine how incredibly deceived mankind will be? Jesus Christ will return to the earth, and the world's leaders and their armies will attempt to fight against Him.

But the day of the Lord will come as a thief in the night, in which the heavens will pass away with a great noise, and the elements will melt with fervent heat; both the earth and the works that are in it will be burned up.

—2 PETER 3:10

20

The Day
of the Lord

ONE OF THE major characteristics of our day is "pseudo-sophistication." In their pride, men and women assume that if they have the right look then they are sophisticated and have it made. In our culture, image is everything—people strive to wear the right pair of sunglasses, drink the latest beer, wear designer jeans and drive the most popular car. Just open any magazine, and you will see the constant appeal to image, style, sex and power.

It is so easy to get caught up in what the Bible calls the "world system." The apostle Paul warns us, "And do not be conformed to this world, but be transformed by the renewing of your mind, that you may prove what is that good and acceptable and perfect will of God" (Rom. 12:2).

Did you ever rent a movie made twenty, thirty or forty years ago and play it on your VCR? Or have you ever watched a black-and-white television commercial made in the 1950s? It's hard to believe that people took themselves seriously back then. The clothing styles, mannerisms and expressions seem so quaint and silly. Yet that's exactly how people will look at our lives a couple of decades from now. However, at the moment people are so caught up in the style and belief systems of our day that they lose an eternal perspective.

The news media, celebrities, personalities and political leaders of our day do not take the Bible seriously. In fact, they label people who believe in the Bible as "right-wing religious fundamentalists." People who believe in the Second Coming of Jesus Christ and in the prophecies of the Bible are thought to be religious "crazies" who are paranoid.

In 2 Peter, the apostle Peter tells us that in the last days people will scoff, laugh and disbelieve the fact that Jesus Christ is returning and that the end of the world is at hand.

> Knowing this first: that scoffers will come in the last day, walking according to their own lusts, and saying, "Where is the promise of His coming? For since the fathers fell asleep, all things continue as they were from the beginning of creation." For this they willfully forget: that by the word of God the heavens were of old, and the earth standing out of water and in the water, by which the world that then existed perished, being flooded with water. But the

heavens and the earth which are now preserved by the same word, are reserved for fire until the day of judgment and perdition of ungodly men. But, beloved, do not forget this one thing, that with the Lord one day is as a thousand years, and a thousand years as one day. The Lord is not slack concerning His promise, as some count slackness, but is long-suffering toward us, not willing that any should perish but that all should come to repentance.

—2 PETER 3:3–9

Even though many in the ecological movement are talking about a coming apocalypse, society in general seems to just push those thoughts out of their minds. In addition, the elite class in our society who basically run the media, the educational system, science and industry have rejected Christianity.

Tom Bethell, writing in *American Spectator* magazine, states, "The underlying problem is that Christianity is seen in American ruling class circles as a faintly embarrassing reminder of our own 'extremist' past, something that needs to be watered down and practiced, if at all, in the privacy of one's own home."[1]

I remember as a college student growing up in Queens, New York, and driving to Jones Beach with my good friend Brian. It was the early seventies, and times were different. Brian had an old English car that looked like a Rolls Royce. Both of us had shoulder-length hair, and we were really hung over from the night before of excessive "partying." To this day I remember looking out the window and seeing miles of sand dunes and the ocean waves in the distance while some radio announcer was reading off grim statistics about how our planet was doomed because of ecological disaster.

The Holy Spirit used that announcement to pierce my heart, and it greatly troubled me. It seemed mankind had no hope and that eventually disaster would overtake the human race. What I didn't fully realize is that God was using that despair to bring me to Himself. You see, the human race, you and I, really have no hope apart from God. Whether the world ends or we die, the result is the same. Each of us needs a Savior to rescue us, and that Savior is Jesus Christ.

THE FUTURE KINGDOM

> For unto us a Child is born, unto us a Son is given; and the government will be upon His shoulder. And His name will be called Wonderful, Counselor, Mighty God, Everlasting Father, Prince of Peace. Of the increase of His government and peace there will be no end, upon the throne of David and over His kingdom, to order it and establish it with judgment and justice from that time forward, even forever. The zeal of the LORD of hosts will perform this.
>
> —ISAIAH 9:6–7

This prophecy predicts that the Messiah will reign upon the throne of David. The Bible teaches us that history is moving in a particular direction and will have a conclusion.

The Bible tells us that there will be a future, eschatological kingdom where Jesus Christ will rule and reign over a new heaven and a new earth in power and glory. This will a time when God will establish His "one world government" over the whole earth, and all Old Testament prophecies concerning Israel will have been fulfilled.

The Book of Isaiah describes the rule and reign of Christ on earth:

> There shall come forth a Rod from the stem of Jesse,
> And a Branch shall grow out of his roots.
> The Spirit of the Lord shall rest upon Him,
> The Spirit of wisdom and understanding,
> The Spirit of counsel and might,
> The Spirit of knowledge and of the fear of the Lord.
>
> His delight is in the fear of the Lord,
> And He shall not judge by the sight of His eyes,
> Nor decide by the hearing of His ears;
> But with righteousness He shall judge the poor,
> And decide with equity for the meek of the earth;
> He shall strike the earth with the rod of His mouth,
> And with the breath of His lips He shall slay the
>   wicked.
> Righteousness shall be the belt of His loins,
> And faithfulness the belt of His waist.
>
> The wolf also shall dwell with the lamb,
> The leopard shall lie down with the young goat,
> The calf and the young lion and the fatling together;
> And a little child shall lead them.

The cow and the bear shall graze;
Their young ones shall lie down together;
And the lion shall eat straw like the ox.
The nursing child shall play by the cobra's hole,
And the weaned child shall put his hand in the
viper's den.
They shall not hurt nor destroy in all My holy mountain,
For the earth shall be full of the knowledge of the
Lord
As the waters cover the sea.

And in that day there shall be a Root of Jesse,
Who shall stand as a banner to the people;
For the Gentiles shall seek Him,
And His resting place shall be glorious.
—ISAIAH 11:1–10

When Jesus Christ first came to earth, He struck the wicked in the spiritual realm (Col. 2:15). In His Second Coming, He will literally establish His kingdom here on the earth at the end of the age (Rev. 19:11–16; 20:11–15).

In the above passage from Isaiah, we see a beautiful picture of what this kingdom will be like. Currently those in the radical environmental movement and those who are attempting to usher in a counterfeit to God's rule are attempting to manipulate, through humanistic means, a kind of paradise on earth. But in Isaiah 11:1–10 we see a wonderful depiction of what life will be like during the Messiah's millennial reign.

Other scriptures point to this future eschatological kingdom.

> And in the days of these kings the God of heaven will set up a kingdom which shall never be destroyed; and the kingdom shall not be left to other people; it shall break in pieces and consume all these kingdoms, and it shall stand forever.
>
> —DANIEL 2:44

When Christ returns, the one-world government of the Antichrist shall be destroyed, and all of man's humanistic governments will come to an end. In the New Testament we read that the New Testament saints will rule and reign with Jesus Christ as kings and priests.

> His lord said to him, "Well done, good and faithful servant; you have been faithful over a few things, I will make you ruler over many things. Enter into the joy of your lord."
>
> —MATTHEW 25:23

The Bible teaches us that while we are here on earth we are to be good stewards over what He has entrusted to us. Life is kind of an earth school where we are being prepared to rule and reign with Jesus Christ.

> You are worthy to take the scroll, and to open its seals; for You were slain, and have redeemed us to God by Your blood out of every tribe and tongue and people and nation, and have made us kings and

priests to our God; and we shall reign on the earth.
—REVELATION 5:9–10

Many of the things we are doing here on earth are preparation for that day. This is why it is so important for Christians to be faithful to what God has entrusted to them. We are responsible as believers in Christ to be faithful husbands and wives and godly parents. All believers should pray for others, intercede for those who are in authority over them and share their faith in Christ. These things prepare us for the time when we will reign on the earth.

In the world system of things, true believers in Jesus Christ are not politically correct. It is easy for us to accept the world's definition of what we are as it is presented in the media and by those who do not know Christ. The world says that we are "odd," "out of it," "ignorant," "weird," "wackos" and "lunatics."

As Christians we must get our identity from what the Bible says that we are. God's Word says that as believers in Jesus Christ we are being trained and prepared to be priests and kings who will reign with Christ on the earth. This isn't some cute little religious fable or a story like "Jack and the Beanstalk." Jesus Christ really is going to return, and we have a magnificent part in that.

WATCH IT!

When Paul warns us to be spiritually awake in 1 Thessalonians 5:6, he is telling us to be careful not to allow ourselves to slip subtly into the traps that Satan has laid out for us. We need to guard our hearts actively against being ensnared by sin. As believers in Jesus Christ we need to walk circumspectly in our lives.

This present world system encourages us to disobey God and to let down our guards. With just the push of a button on our remote controls we can open the floodgates of sexual perversion and lust into our hearts and lives. It may be the so-called "adult" movies so easily available in hotel rooms and on cable television. Or perhaps we will slowly stop going to church and stop being submitted and committed to a local body of believers because we are too busy. We may simply stop reading the Word of God regularly and neglect our daily time with Him.

God wants each of us to be sold out to Him. If we have sinned, then we need to ask Jesus Christ to cleanse us from sin. First John 1:7 says, "But if we walk in the light as He is in the light, we have fellowship with one another, and the blood of Jesus Christ His Son cleanses us from all sin." A little later on in verse 9 we read, "If we confess our sins, He is faithful and just to forgive us our sins and to cleanse us from all unrighteousness."

Sometimes believers in Jesus Christ sin and get involved in things they shouldn't. God does not condemn you. He is waiting with open arms for you to ask for forgiveness. He wants you to admit that you have sinned and failed so that He can forgive and cleanse you by His blood. Today, Jesus Christ wants to restore you. He wants to give you a brand-new, fresh start. Open yourself up to God's cleansing power, and allow yourself to be healed and restored.

But concerning the times and the seasons, brethren, you have no need that I should write to you. For you yourselves know perfectly that the day of the Lord so comes as a thief in the night. For when they say, "Peace and safety!" then sudden destruction comes upon them, as labor pains upon a pregnant woman. And they shall not escape.

—1 Thessalonians 5:1–3

21

When They Say Peace and Safety— the Rapture

I F ANYTHING CHARACTERIZES our day, it is the constant cry for peace by people the world over. Several decades ago, Beatle John Lennon, together with his wife, Yoko Ono, "stayed in bed" for peace in a hotel room in Toronto, Canada. At that time, the world's media converged on their hotel room where Lennon gave a press conference and proclaimed the words to his song, "All we are saying is give peace a chance." Many pop culture personalities like Timothy Leary joined John and Yoko in this world-famous press conference. Yet since that press conference, mankind continues to be ravaged by wars in such diverse places as Bosnia, Chechnya, Iraq and other remote locations on the planet.

Even years after Lennon's tragic murder in front of his apartment in New York City where he was gunned down, the voices crying out for peace have not diminished. Nowhere is this constant cry for peace more evidenced than in the Middle East region between Israel and her neighbors.

The purpose of the apostle Paul's teaching was to prepare God's people to live in the last days. He was not trying to create an atmosphere of irresponsibility or fanaticism. He was trying to teach God's people how to live in the last days.

> But you, brethren, are not in darkness, so that this Day should overtake you as a thief. You are all sons of light and sons of the day. We are not of the night nor of darkness. Therefore let us not sleep, as others do, but let us watch and be sober. For those who sleep, sleep at night, and those who get drunk are drunk at night. But let us who are of the day be sober, putting on the breastplate of faith and love, and as a helmet the hope of salvation. For God did not appoint us to wrath, but to obtain salvation through our Lord Jesus Christ, who died for us, that whether we wake or sleep, we should live together with Him. Therefore comfort each other and edify one another, just as you also are doing.
>
> —1 THESSALONIANS 5:4–11

Paul is telling believers to be spiritually awake, sensitive, alert and prepared for the return of Jesus Christ. In other words, Christians should not be spiritually asleep at this time in history. As we see powerful prophetic events unfold in the Middle East, the push toward globalism, the moral breakdown of our society, the increase in earthquakes, plagues and other signs of the times, we are to be spiritually awake.

The children of this world will be partying, getting drunk, involving themselves in sexual immorality, pornography, materialism and the like, while they are blind to the events all around them leading up to the return of Christ. Like the unbelieving world in the days of Noah, they will laugh, scoff and mock about the message of the Second Coming. For them, Christ is going to appear suddenly and unexpectedly like a thief in the night.

In contrast, believers are to put on their spiritual armor and not allow themselves to get caught up in sin. We are to live our lives in holiness and purity by the power of the Holy Spirit. In addition, all believers are to comfort one another and build one another up spiritually. God has given each of us the awesome responsibility of edifying and building up the people He has put into our lives. When we get to heaven we are going to have to give an account of our faithfulness in this area. We'll be asked if we prayed for and uplifted the people God put into our lives, or if we were so self-centered that we missed these divine opportunities.

181

THE COMFORT OF CHRIST'S COMING

The apostle Paul addressed the church at Thessalonica regarding Christ's coming again. The gospel of Jesus Christ first reached Europe around A.D. 49 when Paul was on his second missionary journey. Paul had received a vision from the Lord of a Macedonian man calling him to preach the gospel. After encountering difficulties in Philippi, Paul and Silas traveled ninety miles to Thessalonica. It was there Paul addressed the theme of Christ's return.

Some modern preachers have diluted the power of this message by setting specific dates or specifying certain limits. Paul did not claim to know more than Jesus Himself, who said, "But of that day and hour no one knows, not even the angels in heaven, nor the Son, but only the Father" (Mark 13:32). Paul taught that the suddenness of the coming of Christ should not surprise Christians who are spiritually prepared.

THE RAPTURE FACTOR

In 1 Thessalonians 4:13–18 Paul says:

> But I do not want you to be ignorant, brethren, concerning those who have fallen asleep, lest you sorrow as others who have no hope. For if we believe that Jesus died and rose again, even so God will bring with Him those who sleep in Jesus. For this we say to you by the word of the Lord, that we who are alive and remain until the coming of the Lord will by no means precede those who are asleep. For the

> Lord Himself will descend from heaven with a shout, with the voice of an archangel, and with the trumpet of God. And the dead in Christ will rise first. Then we who are alive and remain shall be caught up together with them in the clouds to meet the Lord in the air. And thus we shall always be with the Lord. Therefore comfort one another with these words.

This passage of scripture teaches us a number of things. First, it teaches us that the dead in Christ shall rise first, and the living will follow them. In verse 17 it says that those who are alive at the time of Christ's coming will be "caught up," or raptured. Although the exact word *rapture* does not occur in the Bible, the term *rapture* comes from a Latin translation of the Bible where this phrase is translated *simul rapiemur cum illis,* from which we get the word *rapture.*

We are to "comfort one another with these words," according to 1 Thessalonians 4:18. This teaching about the Rapture of the church is intended to provide comfort to Christians in the last days. Christians will be "caught up" with Christ when He comes again. The phrase *caught up* comes from the Greek word *harpadzo,* which means "to seize, snatch away, catch up, take by force."

THE TIMING OF THE RAPTURE

One of the greatest concerns I have as someone who teaches eschatology, or what the Bible calls the "doctrine of last things," is that mature Christians seem to fall into

Satan's snare and fight one another over such things as the timing of the Rapture or when "the Day of the Lord" begins. Most students of Scripture would agree that at best our Rapture positions are an interpretive approach to Scripture. We may feel that our position has the weight of scriptural evidence behind it. But we need to be careful not to allow this to be a point over which we would stop fellowshiping with another believer.

I personally believe that a stronger truth emerges from the study of eschatology. That is, that God has absolutely promised to take care of and supernaturally protect His people. God is committed by covenant to take care of His bride, the church. Nowhere in the Bible does it teach that Christians are immune from trials, trouble, persecution, tribulation or martyrdom. It does teach that God will supernaturally strengthen and be with His people in times of trouble and trial. In many cases, God actually delivers His people from trials. But there are other times when God is with us, as He was with the three Hebrew children in the middle of the fiery furnace of affliction.

What concerns me regarding eschatology and any Rapture position is that all of us are going to be in for some surprises. I have seen some people abuse the pretribulation Rapture position and use it as an excuse to become apathetic in a time when God is calling us to courage and spiritual militancy. This is not the intent of those who teach a pretribulation rapture. But like any other Bible truth, it can be abused by spiritually immature Christians.

THE LIFEBOAT MENTALITY

Unfortunately, many in the Christian culture over the last one hundred years have misused teaching about the "Rapture," turning it into a kind of "lifeboat" mentality. There are some people who use this teaching to justify a position of apathy and noninvolvement in the culture around us. They say that the world is going to get worse and worse, and there is nothing we can do about it. They refuse to get involved in politics and culture and have surrendered our nation into the hands of those who hate God.

A clear understanding of the Bible does not teach escapism and fatalism. God's people are here for a purpose—to occupy until He comes. None of us know when Christ will return. Despite all the prophetic signs on the horizon, Jesus Christ may not return for a hundred years or more. If that is the case, then what right do we have to destroy our children's futures and freedom by a misapplication of Bible prophecy?

OUR FOCUS IS NOT ON ESCAPE!

God's people should rejoice at the prospect of God delivering them from this fallen planet. Our focus should not be on escaping, but fulfilling God's plan for our lives here on earth. You and I have a job to do while we are here. As a body of believers, we have a job to do collectively.

The church is God's representative here on earth, and we are here to do kingdom business until He returns. This means that we are to be living lives of worship to the Lord, praying, evangelizing, raising our children in godliness and interceding. We are to be salt and light in the midst of a dying culture. We are to be fighting actively for our children's futures and doing everything we can to confront powerful forces that are attempting to destroy our nation and planet, both in the invisible realm and on earth. This means participation in the culture, in education, in politics, in the arts, in science and in all other areas. It means not giving our world over to a militant and often antichrist elite, who are attempting to overthrow a Judeo-Christian order.

Who then is a faithful and wise servant, whom his master made ruler over his household, to give them food in due season? Blessed is that servant whom his master, when he comes, will find him so doing. Assuredly, I say to you that he will make him ruler over all his goods.

—MATTHEW 24:45–47

22

....

Who Then
Is a Faithful
Servant?

T HE TEACHING REGARDING the return of Jesus Christ is not intended to entertain us or produce idle speculations about dates and End-Time events. As thrilling as the study of Bible prophecy is and how exciting it may be to see End-Time prophecies unfold, God has intended that the prophetic teaching in the Scriptures both properly motivate us and mature us spiritually. One of the constant themes of the New Testament is our personal accountability before the Lord as the nearness of Christ's return approaches.

God requires each of us to be faithful with the gifts, resources and people He has placed in our lives. In other words, God has given each one of us a job to do before His return, and like an earthly employer He expects us to do that job faithfully. Despite what the world says, we are not our own. We have been bought with a price—the precious blood of Jesus Christ. God expects us to fulfill our duties faithfully.

In contrast, Jesus Christ talks about the servant who says in his heart, "My master is delaying his coming" (Matt. 24:48). This servant does not take his accountability before God seriously. Nor does he understand that his master is going to return soon. As such, this servant "begins to beat his fellow servants, and to eat and drink with the drunkards" (Matt. 24:49). This servant began to treat poorly the people whom God had placed in his life. He actually abused the people God had put in his life.

This truth could speak to us on a variety of levels. Perhaps as husbands we do not treat our wives and children properly. Are we being selfish and self-centered regarding our responsibilities as husbands and fathers? Are we too busy watching football on television or pursuing a career to meet our families' emotional and spiritual needs?

The question is, "Are we being faithful over the people whom God has placed in our lives?"

THE WISE AND FOOLISH VIRGINS

Jesus Christ give us another parable about His return. In the parable of ten virgins, five were wise and five were foolish. Jesus Christ teaches us that the foolish virgins mistakenly thought that the bridegroom was delayed in coming. Then while they slept, "at midnight a cry was heard: 'Behold, the bridegroom is coming; go out to meet him!'" (Matt. 25:6).

The five foolish virgins were totally unprepared for the bridegroom's sudden return. Obviously, the bridegroom is symbolic of Jesus Christ, and the virgins represent members of the body of Christ, or Christians. In this parable the foolish virgins desperately say to the wise virgins, "Give us some of your oil, for our lamps are going out" (Matt. 25:8).

The wise virgins took care of their lamps and of the oil in them. When the bridegroom came they were ready, and they went into the wedding with him. However, the door was shut on the foolish virgins, and they were not allowed to go to the wedding.

This passage speaks to believers in Jesus Christ to fulfill the words of Jesus Christ when He says, "Watch therefore, for you know neither the day nor the hour in which the Son of Man is coming" (Matt. 25:13). We are supposed to be like the wise virgins who had oil in their lamps. The oil and the lamps represent the work of the Holy Spirit in the lives of individual believers. As wise virgins we are to be spiritually alive, and the light in our lamps should be burning brightly when Christ our Bridegroom returns.

If we are in an active, living and spiritually alive relationship with Jesus Christ when He returns, we will go into the wedding feast. In other words, if our personal relationship with Jesus is alive and we are really walking with Christ on a daily basis, then when He returns suddenly and unexpectedly we will be prepared to go with Him into heaven to enjoy the marriage supper of the Lamb. (See Revelation 19:7–9.)

THE PARABLE OF THE TALENTS

In Matthew 25:14–30, we read in the parable of the talents about a man traveling to a far country who leaves different amounts of money with his servants. The message of this parable is that Jesus Christ expects us to be faithful until His return with the resources He has given us. God expects us to use our resources wisely and to produce a "return" on His investment in our lives. The idea is that "watchfulness" in relationship to the Lord's coming does not mean idleness or speculation. While He is away, God expects that each one of His people will produce a return for His kingdom.

Jesus Christ wants us to have His perspective regarding His return. Thankfully, many Christians here in America are looking forward to the return of Jesus Christ. But, what percentage of these Christians are actually being faithful with what God has entrusted to them? Sad to say, many Christians have become "couch potatoes" who expect their pastors, teachers and evangelists to do all the work. However, Christianity was never supposed to be a spectator sport. Part of the reason our nation and world is in the mess it is in is because ordinary Christians are not being faithful to what God has called them to do.

Jesus Christ and the Scriptures repeat this message of accountability over and over again. Without question, we are saved by faith in Jesus Christ alone. But we are also accountable for what God has given us on an individual level. Not everyone is called to be a pastor, teacher or evangelist. Yet every Christian is called to pray for others, share his faith in Christ and raise his children in the admonition of the Lord.

Make no mistake about it; every aspect of our lives comes under divine scrutiny. The Bible calls us to be faithful stewards of our time, finances, gifts and talents. It is only when we have learned to be faithful with what God has given each of us that we will be able to enter into the exciting adventure God has for our lives.

Walking with Jesus Christ is the most dynamic and incredible adventure a person can have. To live with God on the cutting edge is the most awesome thing a person can do with his life. Climbing Mount Everest, amassing a personal fortune or accomplishing any goal does not compare with the plan that God has for our lives. There is nothing wrong with accomplishing certain goals in life or being successful. But the only way any of us find the full release of our human potential or discover who we really are is by making God our Lord and partner in this life. When a person does that, then life becomes, not a drudgery, but an incredible adventure!

PASSIVITY OR BOLDNESS

I think one of the greatest dangers facing Bible-believing Christians today is passivity. Although a number of Christians are bravely moving forward in prayer and evangelism, reclaiming our culture and standing up for what they believe, large numbers of Christians have retreated from the battle and are passive.

I think it is an indictment of the Christian culture that gay activists have made such significant inroads into our society during the last decade. As host of a live radio talk show here in Southern California, I have seen over ten prohomosexual and antifamily bills being promoted by militant gay activists. Some Christians have bravely stood up against this evil. Such legislation would force our children to be indoctrinated into homosexuality as early as kindergarten. It would force churches and Christian radio stations to stop speaking out on homosexual issues. But the church leadership in Southern California and the vast majority of Christians are apathetic and uninvolved in these issues, even though their passage will force churches to have openly homosexual men and women on their church staffs.

On my program I have had guests like Dr. James Dobson, Pat Robertson, Gary Bauer, Dan Quayle and others speaking out on religious freedom issues. Yet the Christian community remains indifferent and uninvolved.

The Bible says, "The hand of the diligent shall bear rule: but the slothful shall be under tribute" (Prov. 12:24, KJV). Tragically, homosexual activists have been diligent in being active, while many Christians believe it is unspiritual to get involved or have been asleep at the wheel. The result is that Christians are being pushed into the corner of society by militant homosexual groups that are using the courts and the media to further their agendas.

There remains a dangerous silence in many quarters of the Christian community, as if somehow it is "spiritual" to be passive and fatalistic. This nonbiblical belief system is like a poison in the mind that will allow our children to become brutally persecuted if we are not careful. In addition, there is a tendency for Christians to hide out in our own private little subculture, attempting to retreat from the world. The only problem with that is that because of the media and other factors, it is no longer possible to hide. The reality is, there is nowhere left to hide.

The Bible teaches us that "the righteous are bold as a lion" (Prov. 28:1, KJV). What is needed is for a Holy Spirit-inspired boldness to grip the church and for Christians to intelligently, creatively and aggressively move forward in reaching our nation for Jesus Christ. Local Christian churches must be very aggressive in evangelizing the younger generation. In all honesty, I see Mormons, Jehovah Witnesses, Scientologists and other groups reaching out, attempting to win people into their belief systems. But too many Christians seem embarrassed by their faith and seem to hide out in the church. To make matters worse, I see a number of ministries that appear to be brave when attacking their brothers and sisters in Christ about their theology. Yet when it comes to facing the real enemy, they are strangely silent.

When the government in Cologne, Germany, persecuted the Church of Scientology, the Scientologists shot back. The Church of Scientology took out a full page in the *International Herald Tribune* and wrote a letter of protest to Chancellor Helmut Kohl. Hollywood stars like Tom Cruise assembled thirty-three Hollywood "heavies" like Dustin Hoffman, Larry King, Oliver Stone, Gore Vidal and Aaron Spelling to join in the protest. Actresses like Anne Archer and others met with United Nations' groups and with the German government to protect religious freedom. In contrast, the Christian culture too often remains silent and uninvolved.

The hour is extremely late, and we no longer have the luxury of a passive Christianity. As Christians, we must be consumed by a fresh vision of Jesus Christ. Our hearts must literally be set ablaze by the power of the Holy Spirit. Our pulpits, seminaries, youth meetings, Bible studies and Christian gatherings must be characterized by a fervent love for one another and spiritual boldness.

Acts 4:31 states, "And when they had prayed, the place where they were assembled together was shaken; and they were all filled with the Holy Spirit, and they spoke the word of God with boldness." The Bible teaches us that true Christianity is one where individual believers and ministers of Jesus Christ are filled with the Spirit and immersed in the Word of God. The result is that they have the *dunamis*—the dynamite of the Holy Spirit. God's people should be joyous and fearless and should boldly move forward to do God's will. In a nutshell, we should not be afraid of the powers of darkness. They should be afraid of us!

Then I saw an angel coming down from heaven, having the key to the bottomless pit and a great chain in his hand. He laid hold of the dragon, that serpent of old, who is the Devil and Satan, and bound him for a thousand years; and he cast him into the bottomless pit, and shut him up, and set a seal on him, so that he should deceive the nations no more till the thousand years were finished. But after these things he must be released for a little while.

—Revelation 20:1–3

23

Final
Judgments

IMMEDIATELY AFTER JESUS Christ returns to this earth, Satan is going to be bound for a thousand years.

Jesus Christ returns to rule and reign on earth, and Satan is thrown into the bottomless pit until after the Millennium. We do not know where the bottomless pit is located. It is probably in another dimension, perhaps inside the earth. The point is that Satan is locked away in some kind of a cosmic prison where he can no longer attack mankind. In the near future, Satan and the powers of darkness are not going to be allowed to continue their evil efforts at destroying and deceiving mankind.

After one thousand years Satan will be released one

last time to deceive the nations (Rev. 20:7–8). After this, Satan will be cast into the lake of fire forever and ever. Revelation 20:10 states:

> The devil, who deceived them, was cast into the lake of fire and brimstone where the beast and the false prophet are. And they will be tormented day and night forever and ever.

Many who submit to Christ's rule during the Millennium will not truly surrender their hearts to the lordship of Jesus Christ. Satan is allowed one final deception in order to separate real believers from false ones. However, once and for all God is going to remove Satan and cast him into the lake of fire and brimstone.

A lot of people do not realize that God is not playing games. Right now He is being patient, because He is giving mankind an opportunity to repent of their sins and turn to Him. The gospel of Jesus Christ is being preached around the world, and millions are turning their lives over to Jesus Christ. At a certain point, this massive influx of souls will be over at the end of the Tribulation. Jesus Christ is going to return to Planet Earth. He will rule for a thousand years in the Millennium. Then Satan will be released one last time.

There will be no second chances. God is going to remove wicked people from this world and establish a new heaven and new earth. History as we know it will come to a conclusion. Those who have accepted Jesus Christ as their Lord and Savior will enter paradise and live with God forever. A brand-new world is waiting to be born. This is not some cute little religious fantasy. A new world is rapidly coming. God's plan for mankind will be fulfilled. You and I are on the threshold of the greatest adventure we have ever experienced. With Jesus Christ all systems are go!

THE GREAT WHITE THRONE JUDGMENT

> Then I saw a great white throne and Him who sat on it, from whose face the earth and the heaven fled away. And there was found no place for them. And I saw the dead, small and great, standing before God, and books were opened. And another book was opened, which is the Book of Life. And the dead were judged according to their works, by the things which were written in the books. The sea gave up the dead who were in it, and Death and Hades delivered up the dead who were in them. And they were judged, each one according to his works. Then Death and Hades were cast into the lake of fire. This is the second death. And anyone not found written in the Book of Life was cast into the lake of fire.
>
> —REVELATION 20:11–15

Let's face it, this is a very difficult passage of scripture to read. It flies in the face of our entire politically correct and morally relativistic world. It is extremely hard to imagine that people who have consciously and deliberately rejected God will be cast into a lake of fire for all eternity. In our humanness, part of us cries out, "No,

God, this can't be fair!" But we have to remember that God is totally fair and just. If we in our humanity feel such compassion and concern, then God feels this compassion and concern to a far deeper level. For you see, we were created in God's own image. If we are grieved at the thought of people being cast into the lake of fire, God's despair must be even greater than ours.

But we must understand that God has done everything He possibly can to save people from destruction by sending His only begotten Son, Jesus Christ, as the Savior. Yet men and women still choose to go their own way and reject Him. There are great cosmic and spiritual forces at work that our finite minds simply do not understand. When we finally arrive in eternity, we are going to understand this completely.

We don't really understand what the lake of fire is, except that it is a horrible place. The imagery the Bible uses is very precise, and I am sure that the term "lake of fire" describes very accurately what this place will be like. It may well be in another dimension, where people are imprisoned forever with the beast, the false prophet and Satan. God must isolate everyone who is sent into the lake of fire for all eternity, because they have become totally corrupt. None of us understand the true nature of evil and why it must be judged.

People who do not accept Jesus Christ into their lives are spiritually dead, and they have chosen to live in a state of spiritual death forever.

EVERYONE IS ACCOUNTABLE

People in our society falsely believe that they can get away with anything. Serial killers, child molesters, dictators, terrorists and others take this to its logical conclusion. They believe that "nobody is minding the store" in the universe and that you can do anything you please as long as you don't get caught. The Marquis de Sade (1740–1814) helped pave the way for this thinking. He advocated sadomasochism as a perverse form of sexual pleasure. Dictators falsely believe that they can commit mass genocide and get away with it. Corporations think they can manufacture products that are harmful or exploit their employees and that nobody is watching. But, the bottom line is that someone is watching, and a day of divine accountability is coming— a day of final judgment!

GET READY

No one knows the day or hour when Jesus Christ will return. Even though there are prophetic signs happening all around us, it doesn't mean we should put on a camouflage outfit, buy some bottled water and head for the hills. The study of Bible prophecy should never produce fanaticism, irresponsibility or weirdness. In fact, the study of the Scriptures should always make us joyous, sound minded and practical—people who can plan their lives intelligently with God's guidance.

However, every believer in Jesus Christ is to look forward

to the return of Jesus Christ. The apostle Peter talks about the day of the Lord when the elements will literally melt away:

> Therefore, since all these things will be dissolved, what manner of persons ought you to be in holy conduct and godliness, looking for and hastening the coming of the day of God, because of which the heavens will be dissolved, being on fire, and the elements will melt with fervent heat? Nevertheless we, according to His promise, look for new heavens and a new earth in which righteousness dwells.
>
> —2 PETER 3:11–13

People who know the Word of God and have a personal relationship with Jesus Christ should have a different perspective on life. We should not be living in fear because God is going to remove His people supernaturally through the Rapture of the church before this earth is burned up and the elements melt.

The Bible teaches us that although this life is important and there is a reason and a purpose for each of our lives here on earth, at any moment, like a thief in the night, Jesus Christ could return for His people. This entire world system could be thrown into what the Bible calls the Great Tribulation.

Therefore, we should live our lives in holiness and purity before the Lord, because at some point He is going to return for His people, and we should be ready. The idea is that we live each day of our lives in readiness for the return of Jesus Christ. That means we should be living the kind of lives He wants us to be living by the power of His Holy Spirit. Secret sins, unforgiveness, bitterness, lust, envy and disobedience have to go. If we are into these things, we must ask Jesus Christ for forgiveness and to be cleansed by His blood.

The Bible suggests that "looking for" and "hastening the coming" of the day of the Lord are linked together (2 Pet. 3:12). In other words, it may be that our spiritual condition can speed up or slow down the coming of the day of the Lord. In any case, believers in Jesus Christ should not live as those people in the world who are caught up in partying, materialism, sex, entertainment and other things. We are to live on the spiritual cutting edge and be ready for when He returns.

So then, what about you? When the countdown to Armageddon reaches global midnight, will you be ready for the return of Jesus Christ?

Notes

Introduction: Following the Comet's Trail

1. Michio Kaku, *Visions—How Science Will Revolutionize the 21st Century* (New York: Doubleday Anchor Books, 1997).
2. Alvin and Heidi Toffler, "Hat Passing in the Global Economy," *Los Angeles Times,* March 27, 1997, p. B9.
3. Art Bell and Brad Steiger, *The Source,* (New Orleans, LA: Paper Chase Press, 1999).

Chapter 1: Is It the End of the World As We Know It?

1. J. R. Nyquist, "Preparing for the Big One," *Dispatcher,* September 1999, p. 8.

Chapter 2: Stormy Weather

1. Taken from an article in the *Los Angeles Times,* August 20, 1998, p. 8.
2. Maggie Farley, "The Weather Is Going to Extremes in Wreaking Havoc," *Los Angeles Times,* September 11, 1998, p. 5
3. "Planet Watch," *Time Magazine,* August 24, 1998.
4. Curt Suplee, "Nature's Vicious Cycle—La Niña, El Niño," *National Geographic,* March 1999, p. 73.
5. Tom Horton, "Stormy Weather," *Rolling Stone,* March 20, 1997, pp. 63–99.

Chapter 3: Death by Volcanoes

1. David Ewing Duncan, "Volcano When the Big One Hits," *Life*, n.d., 52.
2. Ibid.

Chapter 4: A World Facing Disease Crisis

1. Terrence Monmaney, "World Facing Disease, Crisis Report Warns," *Los Angeles Times,* May 20, 1996, p. 1.
2. Dr. Cary Savitch, "Fighting AIDS by Reporting All Cases," *Washington Times,* March 15, 1998.
3. Stephen Sternberg, "Ancient Anthrax Eludes Modern Vaccine," *USA Today,* February 24, 1998, p. 4D.
4. Monmaney, "World Facing Disease, Crisis Reports Warns," p. 1.
5. Ibid.
6. Amanda Spake, "O Is for Outbreak" *U.S. News & World Report,* November 24, 1997, p. 72.

Chapter 6: Decline of the Family

1. Hillary Clinton, *It Takes a Village and Other Lessons Children Teach Us* (New York: Simon & Schuster, 1996).
2. "Big Sister Is Watching," *Phyllis Schafly Report,* September 1999.
3. B. K. Eakman, *Cloning of the American Mind* (Lafayette, LA: Huntington House Publishers, 1998).
4. Ibid.
5. *McAlvany Intelligence Report,* October 1997, p. 22.
6. Taken from a letter from John Whitehead, founder and president of the Rutherford Institute, 1998.
7. John A. Stormer, *None Dare Call It Education,* (Florissant, MO: Liberty Bell Press, 1998).
8. Eakman, *Cloning of the American Mind.*

Chapter 7: Attacks on Privacy

1. Charles Paul Freund, "Call of the Whites...," *Reason,* April 1997, pp. 52–53.

2. Max Boot, "The Wetlands Gestapo," *Wall Street Journal,* March 3, 1997, p. A18.
3. Deborah Schoch, "Bold Dream for America's Wilderness, California and the West," *Los Angeles Times,* September 13, 1999.
4. Francis Schaeffer, *Plan for Action: An Action Alternative Handbook for "Whatever Happened to the Human Race?"* (Old Tappan, NJ: Fleming H. Revell Co., 1980).
5. Nicky Hager, "Exposing The Global Surveillance System," *Covert Action Quarterly,* January 1997.
6. Ibid.
7. Carol H. Fancher, "Smart Cards," *Scientific American,* August 1996, p. 44.

Chapter 8: Clueless on Terrorism

1. Chip Beck, "Americans Don't Have a Clue," *Los Angeles Times,* August 27, 1998, p. B13.
2. Richard Preston, *The Cobra Event* (New York: Random House, 1997).
3. *Washington Drude Report,* October 11, 1999.
4. Steven Komarrow, "Guard Plan Responds to Bio Warfare," *USA Today,* March 18, 1998, p. 1.
5. Arnold F. Kaufman, Martin Meltzer, George P. Schmidt, "The Economic Impact of a Bioterrorist Attack: Are Prevention and Postattack Intervention Programs Justified?" *Emerging Infectious Diseases Journal,* March 1998.

Chapter 9: Drugs, the Occult and a Declining Morality

1. Debra Rosenberg, "Death of Party," *Newsweek,* October 27, 1997.
2. Nyquist, "Preparing for the Big One."
3. James P. Pinkerton, "It's More Disgusting Than You Think," *Los Angeles Times,* October 5, 1999, p. 15.

Chapter 11: The Origins of the Conflict

1. This information has been gleaned from the teaching of Dr. Jack Hayford, The Church On The Way, Van Nuys, California, June 6, 1999.

Chapter 12: The Antichrist

1. Whitley Streiber, *Transformation: The Breakthrough,* (New York: Beech Tree Books, 1988).
2. Paul Davidson, "ATMs That ID Consumers by Eye to Get Test," *USA Today,* March 18, 1998, p. 1.
3. Source for this information is taken from "Midnight Radio Ostman on the Air—George Metcalf Interviews Charles Ostman," *Mondo,* No. 15, Berkeley, California, October 1996.
4. Ibid.
5. Ibid.
6. Marianne Williamson, *The Healing of America* (New York: Simon & Schuster, 1997).
7. Ben Fisher, "The Healing of America," *Magical Blend Magazine,* March 1998, p. 12.

Chapter 13: NATO, Kosovo and Global Government

1. Tony Perry, "Beat Icon William S. Burroughs Dies at 83," *Los Angeles Times,* August 3, 1997, p. 34.
2. James P. Pinkerton, "Strobe Talbott Leads Toward One World," *Los Angeles Times,* June 8, 1999, p. B13.

3. Bill Powell and Yevgenia Albats, "Follow the Money," *Newsweek,* March 29, 1999, p. 38.
4. NyQuist, "Preparing for the Big One."
5. Paul Richter, "Senate Leaders Beat Retreat—Hubble Nuclear Test Ban Bill," October 6, 1999, p. 5.
6. Bill Gertz, *Betrayal,* (Washington DC: Regency Publishing, 1999), pp. 43–5.
7. Chuck Missler, *Personal Update Newsletter,* March 1996.

Chapter 14: One World—an Idea Whose Time Has Come?

1. Books by Alvin and Heidi Toffler include *Creating a New Civilization: the Politics of the Third Wave* (Washington D.C.: Washington Progress and Freedom Foundation, 1994); *Powershift: Knowledge, Wealth and Violence at the Edge of the 12st Century* (New York: Bantam Books, 1990; *Future Shock* (New York: Random House, 1970).
2. Toffler, "Hat Passing in the Global Economy."
3. This ad appeared in the *New York Times* and the *Washington Post* on February 11, 1998.
4. This speech by John Reed at Georgetown University was televised by CSPAN on September 30, 1996.

Chapter 15: Europe United

1. Fred Coleman, "U.S. Companies Expect Benefits From Euro," *USA Today,* March 23, 1998, p. 3B.
2. Eduardo Cue, "The Far Right vs. Culture," *U.S. News & World Report,* February 1998, p. 52.

Chapter 16: China's Kings From the East

1. John Barry and Gregory L. Vistica, "The Penetration Is Total," *Newsweek,* March 29, 1999, p. 30.
2. William Greider, *One World, Ready or Not* (New York: Simon & Schuster, 1997).
3. John Wheeler, Jr., "Forgotten Prisoners," *Christian American,* June 1996, p. 24.
4. Ibid.

Chapter 17: The Fall of Babylon

1. Art Pine, "Iraqis Seem to Be Leaving Kurdish City, Clinton Says," *Los Angeles Times* September 5, 1996, p. 12.
2. Laurie Mylroie, "Saddam and Terrorism: The WTC Bombing," *Newsweek,* October 17, 1994, p. 30.
3. Ibid.
4. Peter Cary, Mike Tharp, "The Gulf War's Grave Aura—Did Iraqi Chemical Weapons Poison American Soldiers and Sailors?" *U.S. News & World Report,* July 8, 1996, pp. 34–35.
5. Ibid.

Chapter 18: Such As Has Not Occurred Until Now— the Great Tribulation

1. Paul McGuire, KBRT, Craword Broadcasting Network, September 28, 1999.

Chapter 20: The Day of the Lord

1. Tom Bethell, "Saving Faith at Stake," *American Spectator,* April 1997, p. 21.

If you would like to be placed on Paul McGuire's mailing list, or if you would like to have Paul McGuire speak at your church, please write:

PAUL McGUIRE

P. O. Box 803001
Santa Clarita, CA 91380-3001
E-mail: paulcontact@cs.com

You can experience more of *God's grace* & *love!*